Beyond Books, Butts, and Buses

Beyond Books, Butts, and Buses

Ten Steps to Help Assistant Principals Become Effective Instructional Leaders

Rebecca Good

ROWMAN & LITTLEFIELD
Lanham • Boulder • New York • Toronto • Plymouth, UK

Published by Rowman & Littlefield
4501 Forbes Boulevard, Suite 200, Lanham, Maryland 20706
www.rowman.com

10 Thornbury Road, Plymouth PL6 7PP, United Kingdom

British Library Cataloguing in Publication Information Available

Library of Congress Cataloging-in-Publication Data
Good, Rebecca, 1958–
  Beyond books, butts, and buses : ten steps to help assistant principals become effective instructional leaders / Rebecca Good.
    pages cm
  Includes bibliographical references.
  ISBN 978-1-60709-879-9 (cloth : alk. paper)—ISBN 978-1-60709-880-5 (pbk. : alk. paper)—ISBN 978-1-60709-881-2 (electronic)
  1. School principals—United States. 2. School management and organization—United States. I. Title.
  LB2831.92.G66 2014
  371.2'012—dc23   2013044407

♾ ™ The paper used in this publication meets the minimum requirements of American National Standard for Information Sciences—Permanence of Paper for Printed Library Materials, ANSI/NISO Z39.48-1992.

Printed in the United States of America

This book is dedicated to hardworking assistant principals who are so intimately involved in the everyday running of the operational side of the school house. It is my sincerest hope that these steps will inspire you to start carving out time to prepare instructionally for the principal position. The greatest gift you can give yourself is landing in that spot prepared for its challenges by arming yourself as a strong instructional leader.

~

Contents

~

Foreword

Since the publication of *A Nation at Risk* (National Commission on Excellence in Education, 1983), there has been a more or less constant churn of reform efforts in American public education. The standards movement, market-based reforms, 21st-century skills, and the role of technology in education represent some of the more prominent reform efforts over the last half century. While many reformers disagree over the precise nature of the challenges in public education, there is widespread agreement over the need for improving educational outcomes for American students.

In the wake of *A Nation at Risk*, another nationally commissioned report on education was published in 1987 to considerably less fanfare. *Leadership for America's Schools* (National Commission on Excellence in Educational Administration, 1987) made an argument for the importance of educational leadership and called for renewed attention to the cultivation and performance of school leaders. Since that time, the quest for better educational leadership has been a constant on the reform agenda. Generally speaking, there are few who would argue against the importance of improved educational leadership as an important element of any plan to improve student learning.

Our investments in producing better educational leadership, however, are yet to reflect the rhetorical importance that we have assigned to the topic. Efforts at the federal, state, and local levels to develop a generation of school leaders with the capacity to lead improvements in student learning have been underwhelming to date. Moreover, much of our approach to the leadership pipeline reflects a failure to update our thinking and practice around leadership preparation as it relates to the modern demands of the principalship. The title of Dr. Good's book—*Beyond Books, Butts, and Buses*—alludes to this very disconnect.

As a new assistant principal, I was promptly assigned responsibility for administering the National School Lunch Program, maintaining the school's computer inventory, and overseeing the human resources benefits program for the school staff. All three items represented cumbersome managerial tasks, each replete with its own endless maze of paperwork and bureaucracy. These responsibilities were actually well aligned with the historical demands of the principalship, where the effectiveness of school leaders was largely, if not entirely, a question of fiscal, organizational, and political efficiency. What was notably absent from the job description was responsibility for the instructional quality and learning outcomes.

Modern principals are expected to be the lead architects in creating and sustaining a coherent and effective approach to curriculum, instruction, and student learning. School leaders are increasingly judged, not just by their ability to maintain a budget and keep the physical plant in good operating condition, but by the academic performance of their students. Unfortunately, our collective thinking about the role of assistant principals—the primary role that we use to identify and develop future principals—has yet to catch up with the evolving reality of being a principal.

My experience as an assistant principal is, I believe, representative of the majority who have occupied that role. That is, we have all faced the reality of a set of responsibilities that are, at best, loosely connected to the social and intellectual mission of the school. We have all confronted a job description dominated by books, butts, and buses. To the extent that we view the assistant principalship as preparation for the principalship, this reality is highly problematic. In short, the modern assistant principalship is wonderful preparation for a job that no longer exists.

If the central responsibility of the modern principal is that of student learning, then we must make that the focus of leadership preparation. That argument can and should apply to the way that we think about, for example, credentialing and graduate education. Common sense dictates that it should also apply to the way that we approach thinking about the work of assistant principals.

This volume—*Beyond Books, Butts, and Buses*—starts us down the path by speaking directly to assistant principals and arguing that they have an active role to play in making sure that their daily lives are focused on student learning. To this end, Dr. Good's writing has three particular virtues with regard to thinking about and supporting the development of assistant principals.

First, it is straightforward, direct, and pragmatic. Despite my argument that we must find a way to make all leadership preparation about student learning, the short-term reality of assistant principals will continue to be dominated by a daunting array of managerial and behavioral tasks. This book accepts the reality that most assistant principals have little available time and even less energy for rambling philosophical speculation about pedagogy, assessment, teacher development, and so on. This volume offers a concrete entry point filled with actionable strategies that can help assistant principals begin to orient their work around the animating purpose of improved student learning.

Second, Dr. Good frames the role of the assistant principal as fundamentally being about preparation for future leadership. This is an incredibly important point for assistant principals and principals alike. For assistant principals, her argument is accompanied by an imperative to take the task of study and preparation seriously. This means that the most important task that assistant principals must attend to is likely absent from their to-do lists. The implications of her argument for principals are that they must approach the role of the assistant principal with great care and intentionality. Principals must devote significant time to mentoring and developing assistant principals with regard to instructional leadership and student learning. It is no longer sufficient to make all the managerial rigamarole the default responsibility of the assistant principal.

Third and most important, the book implicitly makes an argument for the monumental importance of adult learning in schools. The work of leadership is to increase the volume and quality of learning that takes place in the school. Too often, the conversation begins and ends with students, and we neglect the necessity of attending to adult learning and development. Dr. Good does us a great service by targeting a role in the adult community typically associated with discipline and logistics and helping us to reimagine what it would look like to make the assistant principalship fundamentally about learning. In doing so, she challenges us to think about how we might organize every role in the school around learning.

The challenge of improved student learning has never been more urgent. If we hope to get traction around the challenge of education reform and improved student outcomes, then we must find a way to make our practice match our rhetoric with regard to preparing future educational leaders. Dr. Good reminds us that the starting point for this effort is found not in high-level policy discussions but in the hallways and classrooms of our schools.

Specifically, she provides assistant principals a concrete way to refashion their work and focus it on student learning and their development as instructional leaders. In doing so, Dr. Good challenges us to recognize that getting serious about leadership and learning begins and ends with taking responsibility for how we conceptualize and approach our own work.

—Jim May, School Development Coach, New Tech Network

Acknowledgments

My heartfelt thank-you goes to the many hardworking educators who helped shape this book. Working with assistant principals who juggle operational and instructional duties every day in low-performing schools has opened my eyes to the need to help them become more efficient before reaching the principal position. This book is dedicated to them. I sincerely hope that the points in each chapter will help organize, streamline, and prioritize the job duties such that any assistant principal who is earnest in wanting to become more effective will do so.

Thanks also to Mike Dryden, a rare combination of ex-teacher, now statistician, who understands, because he was once there, the need to have quality personnel on a campus. His genius of using numbers to show how we can improve school is underrated. Your time will come, Mike! Thanks also for editing my chapters on accountability and assessment literacy!

Kathy Williams-Palmer, Cheryl Reagan, and Ruth Wilson all helped edit this book and made me sound smarter than I really am—thank you! Bruce Ellis, executive director of instructional technology for Dallas Independent School District, lent invaluable recommendations to the chapter on embracing instructional technology.

And finally, my greatest thanks to my husband, Tom, for his patience with his overachieving wife, and to my children, for their understanding as well. Thanks, Tom, for getting me that laptop so that I could at least sit in the same room with you while I worked on the book!

INTRODUCTION

~

Prepare for the Principalship

The Top 10 Reasons for Becoming a School Principal:
Lots of cool keys.
Choice of parking spots.
Hot lunch every day.
Free admission to games and concerts.
Neat office where you can read magazines and take naps.
Get to keep teachers after school.
Name often appears in print (usually graffiti).
Never grow old being around young people.
Chance to shape tomorrow today.
KIDS!!

—Unknown

The best teacher is the one who NEVER forgets what it is like to be a student. The best administrator is the one who NEVER forgets what it is like to be a teacher.

—Nelia A. Connors

In today's schools, especially under the intense eye of the 2002 No Child Left Behind Act, time seems to run faster. There is not enough time in a day, nor days in a year, to make sure all our campus operational and instructional systems have their *i*'s dotted and *t*'s crossed. Urban schools especially seem to function in panic mode, spending countless hours preparing for a state test that may save them or defeat them, depending on how they are fairing on meeting adequate yearly progress and their own state's accountability standards. There is never enough time to educate students as deeply as teachers and administrators would like, given that in some states what will be on the state test is not necessarily what is covered by that year's curriculum. Precious time must be used to cover the required yearly curriculum plus the standards on the end-of-year state assessment.

So how can busy assistant principals, who already fill their days with the three *b*'s—books, bottoms (discipline), and buses—find time to become stronger instructional leaders before becoming principals? First, let's define instructional leadership. In today's world, the meaning of instructional leadership is broader yet more intense than it was decades ago. Lashway (2002) states,

> Originally, the role involved traditional tasks such as setting clear goals, allocating resources to instruction, managing the curriculum, monitoring lesson plans, and evaluating teachers. Today, it includes much deeper involvement in the "core technology" of teaching and learning, carries more sophisticated views of professional development, and emphasizes the use of data to make decisions (Deborah King, 2002). Attention has shifted from teaching to learning, and some now prefer using the term "learning leader" over "instructional leader." (p. 2)

For generations, districts have chosen principals from the assistant principal ranks based on reasons other than instructional. If an assistant principal was good at discipline, for example, normally *he* would be selected to the revered position, with the expectation that *he* would magically excel in all areas of school functions.

Today, not only do we have women in the ranks of assistant principals, but they are also being selected as principals with the same expectation—that they will magically "fix" a poor-performing school, often without the school reform training needed to bring increases in campus performance.

Assistant principals must start looking at their role more seriously, as one of preparation for the principalship. Waiting until they are named principal is not a good time to learn instructional leadership skills. Resnick and Fink (1999) write,

> Time on the job as an assistant principal or a principal deepens the gulf [between administrative competencies and instructional ones]. Principals' time is filled by the many demands on them for administrative functions. Like most people, they also tend to gravitate toward doing what they know how to do.

Unsure what to look at or how to intervene when they visit classrooms, principals tend to visit rarely, perhaps only to make required formal evaluations. With their knowledge of teaching growing outdated, they delegate questions of instruction and professional development to others. (p. 3)

Many assistant principals are currently serving under a principal like the one mentioned by Resnick and Fink. The following chapters serve as a guide to help assistant principals increase their current instructional leadership skills so that they do not fall into the aforementioned trap. Doing so will benefit not only assistant principals but their entire school as well!

The term *instructional leader*, as used in this book, means developing an assistant principal's whole self in preparation for the principal position. It is my contention that an assistant principal cannot just become more literate in instructional methodology to make an effective principal. To fully prepare for the principalship, an assistant principal must develop other skills in addition to instructional leadership.

Assistant principals must develop internal discipline (a way of staying current in educational trends), value and actually make frequent classroom observations, learn how to use resources to help develop needed skills, know how to build capacity of teachers and staff, and, finally, learn how to manage reluctant learners on a campus. Finally, assistant principals need to learn how to organize so that they can carry out instructional and operational commitments while balancing a professional and personal life.

The chapters in this book will lead ambitious assistant principals to recognize the skills needed in preparation for the principalship and to work at developing those skills by following the recommendations and practices outlined. In doing so, an assistant principal will become not just a stronger, more well-developed candidate for the principalship but a more internally satisfied one.

A note here: In articles on assistant principals, there is often information about the career assistant principal versus the principal-track assistant principal. The strategies within this book serve both types of assistant principals well. Career assistant principals who become better instructional leaders can only serve as even stronger campus advocates for teachers and students.

In preparation for reading this book, arm yourself with a highlighter and a pen or pencil. Be prepared to take notes in the margin, reread sections, and question what you do not understand. Visits to my website and blog may answer some of those questions. If not, feel free to e-mail me at drbgood@goodtx.com. Chapter 11 contains ways to use this book effectively. One of the suggestions is to use it as a book study with a group of people who share a similar goal of becoming more effective instructional leaders. Another suggestion is to find those people now—do not wait till the end of the book to discuss important points found within each chapter.

You will notice that each chapter is not an isolated concept, given that in education we must weave best practices into an ongoing process of the written, taught, and tested curriculum. It is only in the understanding of this process by *all* the campus stakeholders that improvement in student, teacher, and administrator learning will occur.

~

CHAPTER 1

Step 1:
Understand School
Accountability Systems

The first step to becoming a stronger instructional leader is to make sure that all assistant principals know where their schools are as far as their state and federal accountability systems. Did the school "make AYP," or did it "miss AYP"? Is it an "acceptable" campus according to state standards? If these words are not familiar, then pay special attention to this chapter!

It is important for all campus administrators to understand what is causing schools to be operated in such an intense manner as they are today. Due to the often hectic pace of everyday life on a campus, administrators and teachers both get "self-righteously busy." They forget to stay current with what is happening educationally outside their school doors. Many teachers and even administrators have no idea about the accountability systems that have affected them or will affect them in the next year or two.

Certainly, many campus educators do not understand how serious the consequences are for not meeting federal and state performance standards. Educators lose their jobs when their campuses fail to meet the federal or state accountability standards after a certain amount of time. There is no better time than now to have assistant principals strengthen their instructional skills and help their campuses meet and beat the accountability game.

The drivers in today's schools are the two accountability systems: the federal government's adequate yearly progress (AYP) and the state's accountability system. The two do not often work together, especially when it is time to consider when to reconstitute, redesign, and restructure a campus that has failed to meet the required performance standards.

However, the consequences are eventually the same: Both systems require a campus to be shut down if the measured standards are not met several years in a row. This means moving or terminating the administrators and teachers and possibly sending the students to neighboring schools. These consequences are unpleasant and already happening across the country in campuses where school reform has not been able to take hold.

AYP came from No Child Left Behind (NCLB), a federal law proposed by President George W. Bush on January 23, 2001, not long after taking office. A number of federal programs were reauthorized under NCLB with the intent to improve the performance of American schools in the following ways:

- Increase accountability for states, school districts, and schools by use of performance standards.
- Increase the focus on the performance of nine student groups: all students, White, African American, Hispanic, Asian, American Indian, limited English proficient students, special education, and economically disadvantaged.
- Allow parents to choose which schools their children will attend when their current schools are low performing.
- Reauthorize the Elementary and Secondary Education Act of 1965 to increase the focus on reading.

NCLB was signed into law on January 8, 2002. The effectiveness of NCLB's measures is debated daily, weekly, and monthly in educational and lay journals and newspapers across the country. It is difficult to assess the effectiveness of the act because it applies to all states and each state has its own standards-based summative (end of year) test, so comparisons are not easily performed. The law requires that all public schools must give an annual statewide standardized test to students in Grades 3–11. Some states measure AYP in 10th grade, but most states use 11th grade as their AYP grade.

Schools that receive federal grant funding, called *Title I monies*, must make AYP, which is done by meeting the performance requirements for that year. In Table 1.1, on AYP performance standards, the requirements have increased on not only a regular basis but every year, instead of every 2 years, starting the 2008–2009 school year. The pressure to meet AYP will no doubt double due to these increased standards.

Other requirements for meeting AYP include 95% student participation on testing days and meeting graduation/dropout requirements. When a school that received federal grant money fails to make AYP, it is put on a list of "failing schools," which must be published in the local paper. Parents

Table 1.1 Adequate Yearly Progress Performance Standards (in Percentages)

Target Years	Reading / Language Arts	Mathematics
2002–2003, 2003–2004	47	33
2004–2005, 2005–2006	54	42
2006–2007, 2007–2008	60	50
2008–2009	67	58
2009–2010	73	67
2010–2011	80	75
2011–2012	87	83
2012–2013	93	92
2013–2014	100	100

Source. Texas Education Agency (2011).

are given the option to transfer to another school. If the school does not meet AYP for a second year, then special tutoring must be provided for its economically disadvantaged students. Students in schools that have not met AYP after a certain amount of time who also qualify for free or reduced-price lunch are offered supplemental educational services. As stated by the U.S. Department of Education (n.d.),

> low-income families can enroll their child in supplemental educational services if their child attends a Title I school that has been designated by the state to be in need of improvement for more than one year. The term "supplemental educational services" (SES) refers to free extra academic help, such as tutoring or remedial help, that is provided to students in subjects such as reading, language arts, and math. This extra help can be provided before or after school, on weekends, or in the summer. Each State Education Agency is required to identify organizations that qualify to provide these services. Districts must make a list available to parents of state-approved supplemental educational services providers in the area and must let parents choose the provider that will best meet the educational needs of the child.

Providers of supplemental educational services may include nonprofit entities, for-profit entities, local educational agencies, public schools, public charter schools, private schools, public or private institutions of higher education, and faith-based organizations. Entities that would like to be included on the list of eligible providers must contact their state education agency and meet the criteria established by the state to be considered (U.S. Department of Education, 2012).

Some assistant principals may be assigned the task of overseeing the supplemental educational services program at the campus level, handling the student applications, checking to make sure that students qualify for the program, and helping with the logistics of ensuring that the tutoring vendors that serve the students have a location on campus to provide the service on a regular basis.

Each year that the school misses AYP, there are cumulative consequences. Each year, the same consequences apply, plus new consequences are added, as shown in Table 1.2.

As the depth and breadth of the consequences listed in Table 1.2 are understood, administrators of schools feel a sense of urgency to not miss AYP. But remember: This accounts for only half of what is affecting the campuses. States also have consequences attached to their accountability systems, which do not necessarily coincide with the federal system. Oftentimes, the state's performance requirements will be different from what is required for AYP. It is imperative that all campus administrators be cognizant of their state's accountability system, how it affects them, as well as how it may differ from the federal accountability requirements.

The federal accountability system that the nation has been under since 2002—which has led to the "age of accountability," as so many have called

Table 1.2 Yearly Consequences of Missing Adequate Yearly Progress (AYP)

Missed AYP	School Improvement	Consequence
Year 1	—	Review school improvement plan. Address subgroups not meeting AYP.
Year 2	Year 1	Supplemental educational services
Year 3	Year 2	No Child Left Behind choice transfer with transportation. All parents of students attending a Title I school that does not make AYP for 2 or more years are offered choices for their children's education.
Year 4	Year 3	Corrective action plan—may include the following: • Replace school staff relevant to missing AYP • Implement new curriculum • Decrease management authority at school • Extend school year or school day • Restructure internal organization of the school
Year 5	Year 4	Restructuring—plan for one of the following: • Reopening as public charter school • Replacing school staff, including principal • Entering into contract with a private entity • State takeover • Other major restructuring reform
Year 6	Year 5	Implement restructuring plan
Year 7	Year 6	Continue implementing restructuring plan

Source. Texas Education Agency (2003).

it—is undergoing changes as this book goes to print. The Obama administration has considered and taken to Congress two major changes to NCLB. Under the current law, public schools are rated every year on progress toward a goal of 100% proficiency in reading and math by 2014. Schools that fall short of targets for two consecutive years face impending consequences. Those consequences include a mandate to offer transfers to a better school, as well as a mandate to offer supplemental educational services tutoring.

These two mandates would become options under President Obama's proposal. There would no longer be the label of "failing to make adequate yearly progress" or "missing AYP." The rationale for this comes from the following research: In the 2008–2009 school year, according to the Center on Education Policy (2010), about one-third of schools nationwide fell short of what is known as AYP. The center reported that there were 11 states and the District of Columbia that had 50% or more of their schools missing AYP, with the highest 5 states being Florida, with 77% missing AYP; the District of Columbia, with 75%; New Mexico, with 68%; Hawaii, with 66%; and Missouri, with 63% (although some of this may be attributed to a large variation in state assessment rigor and the move to a common core curriculum [p. 5]).

Due to the large number of missed AYP campuses, the government has recognized that the current consequences will cause an undue number of schools to falter, despite some of them actually showing gains. Because the performance standards continue to increase almost every year, especially in math and science, schools that are showing growth still get penalized for not meeting the performance standards. So in some cases, the federal consequences would punish schools that have actually put in effective reforms and are showing growth each year.

The recommended changes for nonachieving campuses are the following. Five percent of the lowest-performing schools would face radical interventions, including replacing the principal in almost all cases. The next-lowest 5% would be placed on watch lists and forced to take major steps. Another 5% with wide gaps in achievement between disadvantaged and better-off students would be required to take action to narrow them. Although some of these sanctions sound similar to the ones already in place, it would target schools by who is not growing versus how they performed on a single yearly assessment.

A positive change being considered is the recognizing and rewarding of high-performing or high-growth schools. Ten percent of the most successful schools in each state would be rewarded with funding and more flexibility and autonomy. That group would include schools that have high test scores and those that show growth. The campuses in the middle between the low performing and the top 10% would be left alone, as in decades before NCLB. If they did not continue to grow, they would get closer attention. As Arne Duncan, secretary of education, has said, "carrots and sticks across the board" about the proposed changes: "rewards and consequences."

Even if Congress revises the law, changing accountability systems in 50 states will take years. Separately, there is a state-led move to shift academic standards toward a new goal: for all students to graduate ready for college and the workforce. That would mean new curricula and new tests.

President Obama's plan does not address the question of whether to eliminate the 2014 goal of proficiency for all. He will leave that decision up to Congress. Instead, there is a new goal that would be phased in over the next few years: to require all students to meet "college- and career-ready" standards by 2020.

A phenomenon that has hit the campuses in the last few years is that, even when a campus has reached acceptable or even higher performance standards, it still "misses AYP" or becomes unacceptable according to state standards. This happens due to not reaching graduation requirements under AYP and cohort completion rate requirements in state systems. An aspiring secondary-level principal will make it his or her business to make sure that the campus has a structure in place that tracks students after they have withdrawn from the campus.

Here is the key piece that many administrators do not understand. If a student withdraws from a campus, that student will still count on that campus's completion rate or graduation rate until he or she enrolls into another accredited institution. The problem of not tracking students who withdraw at the secondary level does not raise its head for 2 to 3 years, depending on the age of the student when he or she withdraws. However, if 3 years down the road, a campus cannot account for a certain percentage of students as far as where and how they finished their schooling, then it does not matter how well the campus achieved academically; it will still suffer a consequence of not meeting AYP or state completion rate.

What this means for secondary-level assistant principals is that the days are gone of telling a student that he or she is no longer welcome at the school due to constant disciplinary or attendance issues. Shortsighted administrators, who cannot see 3 years down the road due to ongoing campus issues, may lose their jobs on account of not making AYP or state completion *again*. As such, it is imperative that "traditional" discipline methods—used by veteran assistant principals and, unfortunately, taught to new ones—be reexamined for how they may be affecting AYP graduation and state completion requirements.

This minilesson in accountability should more than help any educator, especially an assistant principal, to understand the need for everyone at the administrative level to feel a sense of urgency to help implement the campus's instructional plan. As assistant principals read this chapter, I hope that it creates a need to check on the updates to NCLB. By becoming a better-educated instructional leader, an assistant principal can have a positive impact on increasing student achievement.

~

CHAPTER 2

Step 2:
Stay Current with
Educational Trends

Many assistant principals lose track of current educational trends due to being "self-righteously busy." This phrase refers to those daily crises that keep us from our targeted work. Instead of a day doing classroom walk-throughs, today includes dealing with a disrespectful student, an angry parent, and an inept substitute. Our good intentions to get into those classrooms were once again waylaid. Chapter 6 addresses ways of organizing the day so that it is not completely sabotaged.

This chapter focuses on becoming more literate about current educational trends and best practices that lead to personal professional development, which should be ongoing for every educator. Job-embedded professional development, professional learning communities (PLCs), the need for collaboration, and other best practices are discussed. The chapter also reveals how to make time to read current educational literature and how to get resources in other ways besides paper materials.

One of the most important steps to becoming an instructional leader is to stay up-to-date with current educational trends. Many assistant principals are so busy that they lose track of what researchers say about what works in today's classrooms. The National Association of Secondary School Principals (n.d.) says it best:

> Assistant principals [APs] have traditionally been relegated to management roles, dealing with the daily operation of the school. Scheduling, crisis drills, bus and lunchroom supervision, and student discipline are common tasks for APs. In secondary schools, assistant principals often develop "specific expertise" so the

school will rely on the AP year after year. As a result, APs become pigeonholed, preventing more broad experiences, especially those needed for advancement.

The steps in this book help to combat these findings of being "pigeonholed" into noninstructional areas. It may take some resolution and extra effort to do so, but the reward is priceless, since it means ultimately that teacher learning and student achievement are affected while one prepares to assume the principalship.

As mentioned previously, the first step is to recognize the importance of keeping abreast of current educational best practices. Educational researchers have spent years studying what works in schools. It is time for educators to pay more attention to the research on effective instructional practices.

One simple way to stay current is by reading education journals. Several education organizations publish articles or magazines allowing members to access current literature. Several journals even allows readers to download articles to a computer or audio versions to an MP3 player, found now in most cell phones and even GPSs. Time-efficient, busy educators can listen to educational articles while they drive or do mundane tasks. Check with a local tax expert to see if these journal expenses qualify as tax deductions. Some educational organizations e-mail daily news briefs on what is happening in education across the country, which eliminates the need to go looking for them.

Other ways to stay current with educational practices include study groups, book studies, collaboration over instructional practices, job-embedded professional development, and PLCs. Administrators should model personal professional development so that teachers see it as necessary as well.

Study Groups

Create a study group for reading books and articles addressing a best practice that is part of the school improvement plan. Several study groups can run at the same time—for example, school leaders can attend a group that focuses on innovative practices under consideration for implementation, and content area teachers can attend another that focuses on a promising instructional strategy in their subject.

Book Studies

Organize a book study with other administrators or assistant principals at the campus level or from other campuses. Address instructional or leadership practices in monthly or biweekly meetings. Peers' opinions add dimension and meaning for everyone in the book study, as does sharing similar problems and solutions. These meetings are good networking opportunities as well. Do not forget to bring the new ideas and practices back to the campus. Remember: "It's not knowing . . . it's doing" that counts! See chapter 11 for greater detail on this practice.

Collaboration Over Instructional Practices

Collaborate with grade-level or content area teachers to come up with a solution to a known instructional problem. If the data show that a certain student subgroup is lagging behind the others, that issue could be explored through researching what has worked in other schools with similar demographics.

For example, if the special education or English-language learner subgroup has lower test scores in a certain grade level, do an "action research project" with the teachers from that grade level exploring solutions. One teacher explores solutions on websites that specialize in that subgroup; another checks educational journals for articles on helping this subgroup; and another requests that a district specialist who represents that subgroup come to the school to offer effective strategies. Each person reports in during the prescheduled meeting to discuss strategies and practices. The teachers select a practice to try out in their classrooms and then report to the group how it worked.

Not only is this a hands-on method of staying current with instructional practices, but it also adds the element of implementation, which is often lacking in campus book studies. An assistant principal would be part of the action research and be part of the implementation process by monitoring the teachers through classroom observations as they try out new practices. Over time, teachers will feel supported by the assistant principal, especially if he or she has been part of the action research project from the beginning.

Job-Embedded Professional Development

Job-embedded professional development has been around since at least 1994, but not many educators are aware of this term. Job-embedded professional development is instructional learning that teachers acquire as they go through their daily work activities. It can include discussion with others, peer coaching, mentoring, study groups, and action research in both a formal and an informal manner. Although the U.S. Department of Education's Professional Development Team referenced teachers in its 1994 work, administrators can certainly be expected to acquire learning when they take part in these instructional practices with the teachers.

Job-embedded professional development is a shift from the old-fashioned "sit 'n' get" type of training that all educators have come to dread. Instead of sitting passively while being trained by an outside expert, it is the campus teachers and administrators themselves that become the professional developers. This type of learning takes into consideration how adults learn. Knowles (1973), in *The Adult Learner: A Neglected Species*, makes four assumptions about adult learners:

1. Adults learn best when self-directed.
2. They use past experiences to understand new information.
3. They are ready to learn new information when it is important to them.
4. Adults are problem-centered learners; they want to apply new information to their immediate circumstances. (pp. 45–48)

Job-embedded professional development is built around these four assumptions. This is important for assistant principals for two reasons. One, it builds the capacity of administrators and increases their knowledge base as they take part in the learning with the teachers. Two, it allows administrators to both talk and walk the work. That is, they can support the new learning of the teachers by observing them implement the instructional practice in the classroom. Administrators cannot support what they do not know, so it is important that they take part in the staff's professional development. Taking part in job-embedded professional development is an effective and necessary way of becoming a stronger instructional leader. The monitoring piece of job-embedded professional development is so important that a whole chapter is dedicated to this subject (see chapter 3). More examples of job-embedded professional development include the following:

- Two teachers (or an assistant principal and a teacher) chat about an instructional issue, practice, or solution while watching out for students during a passing period.
- A teacher brings back effective practices from another classroom or another campus and not only implements it but also shares the outcome of the implementation with others.
- A teacher demonstrates a lesson on a standard that the observing teachers' data may have shown needs improvement.
- Teachers study student work during PLCs or collaborative meetings, looking at the level of rigor and, possibly, a more effective way of teaching the concept next time.
- Teachers compare student work and grades on a common assignment and discuss why one teacher may have had more effective instruction, as shown by the results.

Professional Learning Communities

A vehicle through which job-embedded professional development flourishes is a PLC. PLCs are meetings where teachers focus on learning (rather than teaching), work collaboratively, and hold one another accountable for results (DuFour, 2004). PLCs have been one of the mechanisms used to achieve job-embedded professional development through encouraging teachers to discuss data and share strategies in an effective manner.

Shirley Hord, a well-known and longtime advocate for educational change and PLCs, writes that teachers and students both benefit from teachers meeting as learning communities. The benefits for teachers include (a) reduction in their isolation, (b) increased commitment to the school's mission, (c) shared responsibility for the development of students and their success, (d) increased meaning and understanding of the content that they teach, and (e) a higher likelihood that they are well informed, professionally renewed, and motivated to inspire students. Teachers also feel more job satisfaction, experience higher morale, and have less absenteeism. Job-embedded professional development is actualized through building the capacity of teachers and administrators to learn new concepts as they participate in PLCs.

Just as important are the benefits, Hord says, that students get from PLCs: (a) decreased dropout rate; (b) fewer classes "skipped"; (c) lower rates of absenteeism; (d) increased learning that is distributed more equitably in the smaller high schools; (e) greater academic gains in math, science, history, and reading than in traditional schools; and (f) smaller achievement gaps among students from different backgrounds.

Schmoker (2004b) reiterates the need for and lack of best practices such as PLCs. He is clear in what the research is saying about this practice:

> Mere collegiality won't cut it. Even discussions about curricular issues or popular strategies can feel good but go nowhere. The right image to embrace is of a group of teachers who meet regularly to share, refine and assess the impact of lessons and strategies continuously to help increasing numbers of students learn at higher levels. (¶12)

Schmoker also lists researcher after researcher who agree that the collaborative practice emphasized by PLCs must happen to have an increase in student achievement:

> The concurrence on [continuous, structured teacher collaboration] is both stunning and under-appreciated. Advocates for focused, structured teacher collaboration include Roland Barth, Emily Calhoun, Linda Darling-Hammond, Richard Elmore, Michael Fullan, Bruce Joyce, Judith Warren Little, Dan Lortie, Milbrey McLaughlin, Fred Newmann, Susan Rosenholtz, Rick Stiggins,

James Stigler, Joan Talbert, Gary Wehlage, Grant Wiggins, Ronald Wolk and numerous others. (¶7)

It is hard to argue against implementing PLCs when researchers are concurring in study after study that it is an effective practice. Suggesting that this be a practice to be studied for possible implementation on the campus would be a good place to start.

The conversations that take place in PLCs are instrumental in changing teacher practice and are just as important for administrators as they are for teachers. If data show that a teacher has a more effective instructional practice and if it is shared and discussed during a collaborative meeting, then it is the duty of the administrator to hold the other teachers accountable to implementing the practice. When an administrator follows through on monitoring, with paper documentation, if teachers do not implement a best practice despite being required to do so, he or she is helping them "grow or go."

Although the aforementioned activities speak to teachers, assistant principals who are looking to build themselves into more effective instructional leaders in preparation for the principalship must take part in activities such as professional dialogue, professional development opportunities, action research projects, and book and article studies. This is a constant theme felt throughout this book.

~

CHAPTER 3

Step 3:
Increase Instructional
Leadership Capacity

The previous chapter emphasizes that an assistant principal must take part in PLCs or collaborative planning meetings with teachers and in professional development. These actions are not necessarily understood or welcomed by the traditional principal. There are still principals who come from a managerial style of the job, so the first part of this chapter presents a model that focuses on how an assistant principal can to talk to his or her principal about how to increase instructional leadership capacity and take a more active role in the educational plan for the school. The second part emphasizes a different model, one that takes into account a principal who is receptive to the notion of an instructional, action-oriented assistant principal. An easy-to-follow checklist is available after each model is described.

Model 1

How can campus administration increase instructional leadership capacity and allow assistant principals to take an active role in the educational plan for the school, especially when it has not been the culture of the school? The first step is to talk to the principal. How to proceed largely depends on the relationship between the assistant principal and the principal. If the relationship is a formal one, then stick closely to the steps provided.

Action 1
Make an appointment to see the principal, with whoever is the keeper of the principal's calendar. Try to find a solid block of uninterrupted time. Meeting for 30 minutes early in the morning, before life takes on the frantic "get everyone to first period on time" rush, is a good idea. Another idea is a working lunch, where the assistant principal and principal eat lunch while discussing the idea of increasing the assistant principal's instructional role. A reason to give for the meeting might be, "I'd like to talk about increasing my instructional role within the campus so I can help even more with teacher and student achievement." Hard to say no to that!

Action 2
Prepare for the meeting by jotting down some notes on what to say and how to proceed once the principal accepts your meeting request. Notes might include reasons for requesting an increased role (cite research provided in this book), some tentative instructional ideas to implement, and a timeline. Instructional ideas will come more easily once you read all the chapters in this book.

Action 3
Meet with the principal and discuss your request to increase the instructional leadership role. Share the intent of wanting to prepare for the principal role and add to instructional leadership skills by taking on a stronger instructional role within the campus. Begin with the research on how assistant principals must begin now to prepare for the principalship by working more closely with the principal in implementing the campus's instructional plan. Share some ideas on how to do that, and then request feedback from the principal.

Action 4
Listen carefully and take notes on what is being shared. Once the go-ahead from the principal has been received, end the meeting by saying that, based on the discussion, an action plan will be put together, along with a timeline.

Action 5
Send the principal an e-mail with a thank-you for his or her time and attention. Within a couple of days, e-mail or provide a hard copy of the action plan and timeline. This is an important action. Developing an action plan along with a timeline is a needed skill for a principal. This is an opportunity to grow, grow, grow! And one can never say thank you enough. Do not leave that step out.

Action 6

Make another appointment 1 to 2 weeks in the future to update the principal on the implementation of the action plan. This will help motivate you to get the initial implementation of your plan started.

Action 7

Monitor the action plan. One thing that separates the great leaders from the not-so-great leaders is follow-though. If campus administrators would follow through on the implementation of their best practices in a precise and consistent manner, school reform would happen automatically. That it does not happen speaks to the problem that most administrators have—that is, letting themselves be derailed daily from their scheduled plan by unexpected events, parent visits, central office meetings, and so on. Learning how to avoid some of these pitfalls comes in later chapters.

Action 8

Meet with the principal for an update on how the action plan is going. This can be one of the most satisfying steps between an assistant principal and principal. As you go through the action plan, be sure to listen for feedback. Take notes and adjust the plan if necessary. Be ready if the principal suggests a change. He or she is the instructional leader and has the ultimate say on what will happen on the campus.

Action 9

Continue with regularly scheduled meetings with the principal. It is important that the principal knows what is happening and has an opportunity to provide input and feedback. Professional respect between the assistant principal and the principal will deepen while working together in these meetings.

On a personal note, there is a good reason why going to this effort should take place: After several of these meetings or after the implementation of the practice shows that it has built capacity in teachers and led to a change in instruction and, possibly, student achievement, think of the high-quality recommendation letter that the principal will be able to write for the assistant principal when applying for principal positions!

If the relationship with the principal is more friendly and casual, there may not be a need to go through some of the formalities in the Model 1 checklist. However, still take notes about what is discussed, and come up with an action plan and a timeline to share with the principal. Meet regularly to update and receive feedback. Use the following checklist to help you follow through and keep track of the steps that you have implemented.

Model 1 Checklist
- ✓ Action 1: Make an appointment with principal.
- ✓ Action 2: Prepare talking points for meeting based on the information in Model 1.
- ✓ Action 3: Meet with principal and discuss the request to increase instructional leadership capacity by implementing a needed instructional practice.
- ✓ Action 4: Take notes during the meeting.
- ✓ Action 5: Send thank-you e-mail to principal for meeting that day or the next.
- ✓ Action 6: E-mail principal the action plan and timeline within a couple of days.
- ✓ Action 7: Request another appointment two weeks in the future to update principal on the implementation of the action plan.
- ✓ Action 8: Monitor the action plan.
- ✓ Action 9: Meet with principal regularly and provide updates on the implementation of the action plan.

Model 2

There are principals now who understand the necessity to have "all hands on board" when it comes to using all available resources to help implement the campus's instructional plan. Assistant principals are often untapped instructional implementers who are regarded as the managers of the "operational side of the house," so to speak, letting others deal with curriculum and instruction. With a different expectation, assistant principals can get the traditional three *b*'s done—books, butts, and buses—and add instructional capacity to oneself, teachers, and students.

Model 2 recognizes that there are principals who are aware of the need to use all existing personnel to help implement and monitor the campus's instructional plan as documented in the school's campus improvement plan or school improvement plan. This type of principal gathers the administrators early in the school year to discuss the organizational structure that their team will form and follow.

A possible structure might be that the principal assigns a content area to each campus administrator. On a campus with one assistant principal, the breakdown might be what is seen in Table 3.1, and on campuses with more than one assistant principal, the breakdown would be determined by the number of administrators and their expertise areas.

Table 3.1. Administrator Assignments

Administrator	Content Areas	Other Duties and Responsibilities
Principal	Math Social studies	Limited English proficiency, electives, professional development Bus/lunch duty, Parent–Teacher Association, site-based committee
Assistant principal	Science Reading/language arts	Special education, discipline, textbooks Bus/lunch duty

If there is an assistant principal with a strong science background, then it would make sense to assign that person that content area. Any time that teachers have an administrator who comes in "talking the walk," it makes the practice more credible. However, even when there is no one who has a strong content background in areas such as math or science, an administrator must still be assigned. Said administrator must go into this with an "I can learn" attitude.

One of the ways for an assistant principal to become more comfortable with a content area is to use the available district scope and sequence or curriculum guide for that subject. Study the portion that corresponds with the period, for example, the first 6 weeks. This way, when attending the PLC meetings, questions can be asked, such as "I noticed that the Pythagorean theory is to be taught next week. What methods will you use to teach it? Are there any hands-on opportunities? Where's the rigor? How will you make this culturally relevant to your African American and Latino students?" These questions will lead (hopefully) to lively answers from the team of math teachers teaching this concept. This type of discussion, facilitated regularly by an administrator, will buy teacher trust and credibility. Moreover, the assistant principal can now easily monitor what was discussed.

Another way to monitor a content area with no content expertise is to have district-level content specialists come to the content meetings on a regular basis to help check on the rigor of the practices. Attending professional development in that content area is a must for the administrator, since the strategies shared at the workshops can be easily looked for during classroom visits upon returning to the campus.

Taking "impact walks" with teachers from that content area is another way of building capacity as teachers discuss what they observed. More discussion about impact walks is addressed in chapter 4.

Once administrators are assigned content areas and other responsibilities, the next part of the Model 2 structure involves weekly meetings with the principal and assistant principals to discuss what was learned and monitored that week. The practice of meeting regularly to share what is going on in the content areas is as important as the going into the PLCs and the classrooms. For this to work at maximum speed and efficiency, the principal must monitor the ministructures or the arrangement of curriculum activities for the content areas facilitated by the administrators. Textbox 3.1 is a sample of an administrator meeting agenda.

Textbox 3.1.   Sample Agenda for the Weekly Administrator Meeting

Weekly Administrator Meeting

Date:
Attendees:

Weekly Share-Outs
Classroom walk-throughs:
  Data: How many done? Weekly goal met? Evidence?
  Overall summary (with evidence):
  What patterns do we need to address as a team? Evidence?

Teacher in need of assistance:
  Any new teacher growth plans? Evidence?
  Are the teachers currently on growth plans showing improvement? Evidence?
  Any other personnel issues to discuss?

Specific Subgroups
Administrator over special education:
Special education—do we know who is taking which test? Which accommodations will they use?
Are inclusion teachers following their inclusion schedule? Evidence?
Are mainstream teachers following the individual education plans? Evidence?
Is there a list of struggling special education students with interventions? Evidence?
Are they attending tutoring? Evidence?
Are inclusion teachers tutoring? Evidence?
Are there students that an administrator needs to call home on due to lack of progress or lack of attending intervention?

Administrator over English-language learners:
Do we know who is exempt? Who is taking which test and what accommodations are needed?

Is Monthly Language Proficiency Committee meeting? Evidence?

Is there a list of struggling English-language learners with interventions? Evidence?

Are they attending tutoring? Evidence?

Are ESL teachers tutoring? Evidence?

Are there students that an administrator needs to call home on due to lack of progress or lack of attending intervention?

Administrator over subgroups:

Are teachers tracking their struggling learners by subgroup? Evidence?

Are interventions being made available? Are they working? Evidence?

Are there students that an administrator needs to call home on due to lack of progress or lack of attending intervention?

Upcoming professional development:
  Based on what need?
  Based on what evidence?
  Topic:
  Date:
  Presenter:

Share-out on last week's learning walk:
  Focus and content area:
  Any professional development concerns based on classrooms visited?
  Upcoming learning walks:

Discipline issues:

Miscellaneous items:

Teacher grades—have teachers been inputting the required three grades a week?

If not, who received letter of omission? Reminder: Three omission letters = a memo from the administrator over that subject.

Lesson plans:
  Any concerns?

Attendance Committee meeting:
  Teacher attendance issues:
  Student attendance issues:

Other:

Book/article study:

Notes:

The principal becomes the final monitor of the ministructures, making sure that the assistant principals are monitoring their content areas and the subgroups within those content areas. That monitoring takes place in weekly administrator meetings, where each administrator shares out his or her areas, and in visual inspections of hard evidence.

Evidence can take the form of an administrative binder that has tabbed sections. Each section contains evidence, such as agendas, sign-in sheets, and notes from meetings. It can also contain walk-through or growth plan documentation, parent contact log, weekly calendar, and so on. The principal will not only hear the sharing of information but also look for hard evidence that this is actually happening. A good principal who does this will have few end-of-year surprises, because the assistant principals were monitored to do what they said they were going to do. This culture of follow-through can be fostered only by the principal's commitment to ask for weekly evidence. The following is an example of a mini-structure from Campus A.

On Campus A, there is an assistant principal who is over both the special education department and a content area. That administrator makes sure that (a) the special education teachers are following the inclusion schedule; (b) the admission, review and dismissals are completed in a timely manner; and (c) the School Support Committee (usually manned by the campus counselor) intervenes for the struggling students who are at Level 3 of the pyramid response to intervention.

The assistant principal, who also has a content area, say social studies, monitors whether the inclusion teachers (a) come to the PLC of the content area they are supporting, (b) walk around during social studies class helping all students in the classroom, (c) do not sit next to the special education student the whole period (which points that child out to the rest of the world as the special education student, a big no-no due to confidentiality issues), and (d) follow up on the interventions that those students should be receiving.

The same assistant principal follows up with the other campus administrators, asking if they are seeing their content's inclusion teachers following the inclusion schedule and monitoring all students. That way, he or she is monitoring the inclusion teachers in all content areas through the eyes of the other administrators. The assistant principal then follows up if another administrator mentions that the math inclusion teacher has not followed the inclusion schedule this week. There may be a legitimate reason for the teacher not being there, but the culture of monitoring begins to take hold.

If the campus has adopted the coteaching model, where the inclusion teacher plans and coteaches with the general education teacher, the administrator monitors that as well. Of course, the assistant principal would also monitor all the social studies teachers as far as classroom observations, PLC attendance, and so on.

These structures might be seen as overlapping, and that would be correct. Just as some of the information in these chapters overlap, the instructional structures must weave seamlessly together so that there are always more than one set of eyes checking to make sure that the structures, as agreed on with the principal, are being implemented.

One must "inspect what you expect" to ensure that best practices are being carried out and to periodically check if they need tweaking due to a lack of measurable success. Implementation of this begins with the principal monitoring the assistant principals, the assistant principals monitoring teachers, teachers monitoring students, and students monitoring themselves. This not only is doable but is being done in high-achieving campuses.

Before this structure is implemented, it will be important for the principal to hold a meeting with the administrative staff to explain it. Talking points might include the following:

What roles and responsibilities each administrator will carry out on the campus. A handout of that should be made available to the teachers so that they know whom to address in what area.

What content areas each administrator will be over and the duties required during the instructional day. Those tasks might include the following:

- Facilitate each team meeting.
- Help develop an instructional calendar for that content area.
- Make sure that the meetings department chair has an agenda, sign-in sheet, and meeting notes.
- Ensure that the instructional calendar, agendas, sign-in sheets, and meeting notes are kept in an instructional binder, easily accessible to other administrators and visitors.
- Arrange for professional development for the content area teachers as noted by current assessment results. This can be done by consulting with the department chair, the district content specialists, the principal, and so on.
- Attend the content area professional development (remember—one cannot support what one does not know!).
- Have weekly checks on the students who are receiving pyramid response to intervention. The assistant principal would ask questions such as "How have the interventions worked for Janice so far?" "Is Manuel coming to weekly tutoring?" "Whose parents do I need to

call this week due to behavior or not coming to tutoring?" "Where is the list of students who you think will not pass the state assessment without major interventions?" "What are we doing with that group that is over and above the others?" "How are our subgroups doing?" "How do you know?"

- Arrange and attend impact walks with teachers on a regular basis to measure the impact of the recent professional development (see step 4 on impact walks).
- Follow up with teachers who are in need of assistance by putting them on a growth plan.
- Monitor growth plan every 3 weeks until assistance is not needed anymore.
- Mentor at-risk students in that content area.
- Call parents of students whom teachers have identified as at risk due to lack of performance, homework, attending tutoring, and so on.

How the principal will oversee the structures by meeting weekly with the administrators for operational and instructional areas debrief.

Suggestions on how to manage this type of schedule.

Yes, some of these suggestions seem to be more principal-led practices than assistant principal ideas, but on some campuses, it may take a forward-thinking assistant principal to bring the idea to the principal, rather than the other way around. Here is a checklist to help keep the suggested actions in mind:

Model 2 Checklist
- ✓ Action 1: Make an appointment with principal to talk about implementing the Model 2 structure (if not already in place).
- ✓ Action 2: Prepare talking points for meeting based on the information in Model 2.
- ✓ Action 3: Meet with principal and discuss the request to increase instructional leadership capacity by implementing a Model 2 structure.
- ✓ Action 4: Take notes during the meeting.
- ✓ Action 5: Send thank-you e-mail to principal for meeting, and share enthusiasm for the plan.
- ✓ Action 6: Principal holds faculty meeting to discuss the new administrator structure.
- ✓ Action 7: Assistant principal attends his or her content area PLCs and does frequent classroom observations and walk-throughs.

✓ Action 8: Assistant principal shows evidence of Step 7 by bringing a binder with the classroom observations, teacher growth plans, PLC agendas, sign-ins, and meeting notes to the weekly administrative meeting.

The important thing here is doing what is best for "the little people." When decisions are made because it is convenient for the big people . . . that is when the focus becomes less clear. Remember: A principal is not magically transformed into a successful school leader overnight. He or she must become that by working the steps outlined in this book while still an assistant principal.

CHAPTER 4

~

Step 4:
Set a Walk-Through Goal

For the last several decades, campus administrators and teachers have used the classroom observation as an evaluative tool to be endured once or twice a year. Most districts require a formal evaluation to be completed toward the end of each school year.

A normal scenario comprises an administrator who walks into a classroom around March or April, with a pad or a form, and sits down to observe for about 45 minutes (usually the minimum time required each year for a formal evaluation). A year's worth of professional opinion on the effectiveness of the teacher is generated from that one visit.

The administrator, many times not well versed on effective instructional practices, gives a *proficient* or *exceeds expectations* score, and the teacher and the administrator forget about the whole experience until it is repeated the following year. The problem with this model is that both players walk away without having learned anything about how to be a more effective educator.

This chapter shows why it is necessary to set a goal to do weekly walk-throughs. The research behind goal setting and the role that motivation plays are also shared. Different types of walk-throughs are discussed along with effective teacher feedback. Useful templates and checklists are included, which can be found in appendix G.

The Need to Set a Goal

The research literature is clear in the need to set goals. Goal setting is a powerful way to motivate people. The value of this activity is so well recognized that corporations would never neglect to have goal setting as part of their yearly company plans. Any good organization has goal setting incorporated within it.

Mindtool.com quotes Dr. Edwin Locke's (1968) pioneering research on goal setting and motivation: "goal setting theory is generally accepted as among the most valid and useful motivation theories in industrial and organizational psychology, human resource management, and organizational behavior" (¶3). To do this, many school districts have begun moving toward the use of SMART goals.

Goals that are SMART are specific, measurable, attainable, relevant, and time-bound. It means that the language used to write out the goals is specific and measurable. The goals must be attainable and relevant to the goal setter, and they must have a realistic time frame as far as their accomplishment is concerned (Mindtools.com, n.d., ¶4).

Many organizations, including educational ones, have found that goals are easier to accomplish when they follow these simple steps. Locke's research shows there is a relationship between how difficult and specific a goal is and people's performance of it. He found that specific and difficult goals led to better task performance than vague and easy goals. Using phrases such as "Try hard" or "Do your best" is less effective than "Try to get more than 80% correct on your next test" or "Concentrate on beating your last score."

Having a goal that is too easy is not a motivating force. As hard as it may be to believe, difficult goals are more motivating than easy goals because it is much more satisfying to accomplish something that effort has been put into.

After Locke published his article on the need for goal setting in the 1960s, another researcher, Dr. Gary Latham, studied the effect of goal setting in the workplace. Latham's results supported exactly what Locke had found, and the inseparable link between goal setting and workplace performance was forged.

There are two types of goals: *proximal goals*, which are short-term achievable goals, and *distal goals*, which are long-range goals. Challenging proximal goals serve as benchmarks toward distal goal mastery, intrinsic interest, and a growing sense of self-efficacy. In other words, success with short-term (proximal) SMART goals serves as road signs along the academic journey toward the long-term (distal) goal.

As the goal setter achieves success on each proximal goal, he or she continues to be intrinsically motivated to continue the effort. As he or she continues the effort, new behaviors are formed. When the goal setter meets the distal goal, the validity of those behaviors is reinforced. Learners become self-regulated when they become active in their own learning through goal setting. In an effective organization, whether a district, a school, or a classroom, short- and long-term goal setting should be an ongoing expectation.

The Role of Motivation in Learning

Administrators who understand how to nurture and develop intrinsic motivation consistently increase teacher motivation. Educators need to understand the construct of self-efficacy as an important factor in classroom performance and motivation. Self-efficacy—the power or capacity to produce a desired effect or effectiveness—also contributes to intrinsic motivation (Bandura, 1993).

As people develop beliefs in their abilities, they challenge themselves to higher goals and, in turn, enhance and sustain intrinsic motivation. Those with high efficacy learn to exercise control over stress, anxiety, and the demands of their academic programs. As found by Yingling (2003), self-efficacy has a positive influence over psychological well-being and functioning. This can be applied to students as well.

Educators tend to predict achievement based on student ability and ignore the affective domains, such as self-efficacy, self-regulation, and motivation. If this can be turned the other way and needed attention put to the affective domains, the accuracy in predicting student achievement will increase.

Goal-Setting Alignment

Imagine a campus that puts the following campuswide goal-setting alignment into place. Begin with students' goals that align with the teachers' classroom goals. Those teacher goals would align with the grade-level content goals, which would align with the campus content goals. Each content area displays its goals in the classroom, hallways, and entrance of the school in the form of graphs and posters.

Why put this into place? Why go to this degree? There are several reasons. Positive things occur when goal setting is taken to this level. Healthy competition occurs when goals are set in attainable measures. Campuses that involve their students in student self-management of learning ignite interest and value in the testing process. For example . . .

Goal setting by student leads to

- Students who become more intrinsically motivated to alter their behavior so they can see the increase in performance enough to meet their personal goals
- Teachers who become more intrinsically motivated to ensure that their students are getting what they need to reach their personal goals

Goal setting by classroom leads to

- Students who hold one another accountable to alter their behavior so they can see the increase in performance enough to meet their classroom goals
- Teachers who become more intrinsically motivated to ensure that their students are getting what they need to reach their classroom goals
- A natural and healthy competition among class periods when scores are posted and compared

Goal setting by campus leads to

- Students who have heightened awareness of school goals when they are posted in the hallways
- Parents and other school community partners who are alerted of the upcoming major assessment goals, because they are posted in the school entrance and other heavy-traffic areas, such as the cafeteria and the library
- The principal and the faculty urging parents and other school community partners to "help us meet our goals" through tutoring, mentoring, and so on, during Parent–Teacher Organization or Parent–Teacher Association meetings and other campus-related events

At every level,

- There is the ongoing opportunity to celebrate the reaching of goals!

When a campus can involve the whole school community in working toward meeting the set goals, imagine how empowering that is for everyone.

Think of the celebration when the goals are met. Campuses do not celebrate often enough: It is through the celebrations that everyone gets renewed and energized enough to tackle the next goals.

Recall that formative assessments often test different standards each time they are given (since they test what was recently taught), so goal setting cannot always be done by standard. It can, however, be done by behavior. For example, a student can write as part of one's goal-setting plan that he or she will be more consistent in attending tutoring, handing in homework, paying attention in class, and arriving to class on time.

Any student who not only agrees to do this on a signed goal-setting form but then actually follows through with these behaviors will perform more successfully on any given task. It may take some help on the part of the teacher to remind the student what he or she has agreed to, but the result will be worth the effort.

How does all this affect an assistant principal? If goal setting is not currently part of a school's campus improvement plan, it would be a good project to take to the principal in either Model 1 or Model 2 as mentioned in chapter 3. It is also necessary for administrators to monitor the implementation of this plan of action by (a) making sure that goal setting is on the PLC agenda after a formative assessment has been given, (b) sitting in on the PLCs to make sure that it is addressed effectively, and (c) monitoring the use of goal-setting tools by teachers with students in the classroom. "Inspect what you expect," and it shall happen. Assuming, without evidence that it is happening, leads to implementation by "pockets of excellence," with not enough excellence most of the time.

Human psychology being what it is (similar to "what gets tested gets taught") leads to the belief that if teachers know that goal setting is faithfully monitored, it is more likely to get done. The vehicle through which the monitoring occurs is the classroom walk-through.

Types of Classroom Walk-Throughs

This book shares four models of walk-throughs. There are many variations of walk-throughs, and by no means is it being suggested that the following models are the only ones through which teachers should be observed. The walk-throughs listed in this book are but a small sampling of the types of walk-throughs that can be found. Different districts or campuses have a variety of walk-throughs and forms that are used successfully to help teachers grow. It may be necessary to apply the concepts from this book to the tools and templates used by your district. There is no right or wrong type of walk-through or form. The important takeaway here is that (a) a goal should be set for weekly visits, (b) a form allowing feedback should be used and returned to the teacher in a timely manner, and (c) the feedback should be positive where possible while looking for areas of growth opportunities for the teacher.

The models presented here are to be used all year, not just once or twice like the more formal evaluative walk-through that is needed to satisfy a district's teacher evaluation process. The four models that are discussed help build instructional capacity in teachers and administrators in preparation for the end-of-the-year formal evaluation.

The four models are the 1- to 3-minute walk, the focus walk, the speed walk, and the impact walk. They each have slightly different reasons to be used. A savvy administrator uses a combination of these walks during the school year as the need arises. The 1- to 3-minute walk should be the standard walk-through, as it allows the administrator to pick up on patterns and trends that are occurring in the classrooms that he or she visits every few days.

One- to Three-Minute Walks

This walk-through needs to be done often. If between 1 and 3 minutes are spent in a teacher's classroom every few days, an administrator will begin to notice and document patterns and trends occurring. These could include a lack of student engagement, too many worksheets, not transitioning in a timely manner from one instructional stage to another, lack of rigor, not doing differentiated instruction, lack of bell-to-bell instruction, and so on. These walk-throughs allow for constant and quick redirection through teacher feedback, especially early in the school year, so that the issues being seen by the visiting administrator will not have a strong or lasting impact on the students.

For example, let's say that over a 2-week period, an administrator has observed during the last four visits to a certain classroom that a teacher has been lecturing from the front of the room. That administrator would have a conversation with the teacher about what other instructional strategies he or she might use instead of lecture.

If the teacher was not sure about what other instructional methods to use, then the administrator would make professional development suggestions, such as observing another teacher, assigning professional teaching videos to watch, and so forth. The administrator might also consider placing the teacher on a growth plan to ensure an ongoing conversation between them. The key is to have the 1- to 3-minute walks be a regular thermometer of what is going on in a set of classrooms.

This type of walk-through is also valuable as far as noticing patterns and trends in a series of classrooms over a given period. Let's say that an assistant principal is over the English language arts and reading content area. He or she observes that over the last 2 weeks, the teachers in the same grade level do not seem to be following the instructional practices discussed and agreed on in the PLC. This should lead to a conversation between those teachers and the visiting administrator in the next collaborative opportunity as to why the practices that everyone agreed were rigorous and relevant are not being carried out in the classrooms.

Focus Walks

Focus walks target a specific area for the administrator to look for as he or she goes into a classroom or series of classrooms—such as (a) implementation of a campus or district initiative, (b) evidence of the latest professional development training, (c) the level of student engagement or participation in hands-on activities, (d) rigorous and relevant instruction, (e) transition between instructional stages, (f) teacher questioning techniques, (g) bell-to-bell instruction, and (h) "wall walks" (what is on the classroom walls? does the environment show what concept is currently being studied? is it a print-rich environment?). These are all good examples of focus walks.

After the assistant principal has settled on what the focus of the walk will be, possibly during a discussion with the principal, he or she announces what it is during the next PLC. Teachers and the administrator share what the evidence of that practice looks like, so there is a clear understanding that these walk-throughs are not a "gotcha" but instead an opportunity to grow for teachers.

After the focus walk is over, the assistant principal meets with the teachers to debrief. Feedback is the most important and most neglected part of most walk-throughs, so it is important that it happens. The feedback can be in an informal or formal setting; as such, using a passing period while teachers are out monitoring the hallway can be a doable setting if the information is not too critical. Following up with an e-mail about the conversation, especially if it was about a needed change, is always a good idea. Courtesy e-mail messages turn into solid documentation when and if needed.

After giving the feedback on a needed change, mention to the teacher that you will be looking for evidence of this change in the next few days—then, do so. With luck, the next debrief will be one of celebrating the implementation of a more effective practice.

Speed Walks

A speed walk has three parts that involve an administrator spending 5 minutes at a time in a classroom or series of classrooms during one instructional period. The first 5 minutes is spent at the beginning of the period when the administrator documents what is going on instructionally at that time. During the second 5 minutes, the administrator returns in the middle of the period and documents what is going on instructionally at that time. The last 5 minutes is spent at the end of the period when the administrator documents what is going on instructionally as well. An observation tool for a speed walk is found in appendix G.

This type of walk-through is an excellent tool to use to answer a variety of issues and questions. Sometimes, a teacher mentions after a walk-through that, had the assistant principal come earlier or later, he or she would have seen whatever was missing according to feedback on the returned form. A speed walk can help answer some of those complaints.

Oftentimes, especially with new or struggling teachers, this type of walk-through can help an administrator see if a teacher is pacing himself or herself correctly when it come to bell ringers or warm-ups at the beginning of the class, transitioning from teaching the concept to independent study, and teaching bell to bell.

Impact Walks

An impact walk measures the effect that a recent district or campus professional development session had on teachers by visiting a series of classrooms a few weeks later. It is important to note here that this walk is nonevaluative. The feedback from the walk should be about whether the recently received professional development can be seen in some way implemented in the classrooms visited.

If the teachers took part in a session on rigorous instruction, for example, can that be seen in the classrooms now being visited? Before an impact walk takes place, the team of people who will be doing it talk about what type of evidence they will be looking for. It could be that they would look for rigor not only in the type of instruction going on but also in the student work posted on the walls. They might ask students questions about the current concept being taught. If the students' answers have depth, then that could be considered as evidence that they have been exposed to rigorous instruction, even if it was not viewed by the observers at that time.

It takes practice to bring feedback from the classrooms in a nonevaluative manner. Statements such as "I didn't see much student engagement" are replaced with "Might the teacher need some type of graphic organizer to help the students understand that concept better?" or "Although we have given professional development on higher-level questioning, I didn't hear much use of it in the three classrooms we visited. We may need to repeat the training and go over it again in a different way."

It is imperative that a structure be in place on a campus to measure the effectiveness of the recent professional development. Impact walks can be that vehicle through which this can be measured. A sample of an observation sheet that could be used for impact walks can be found in appendix G.

Another document that should be kept by the administrator over the content area and shared every few weeks at the weekly administrator meeting is the continuous observation log for impact walks. Appendix G shows an observation log that has been partially filled out. In this log, the administrator continually reviews the implementation of the campus's professional development, logging in not only the observed results, but also possible suggestions to bring to the weekly administrator meeting.

Keeping track of what is seen during walk-throughs and then what is being done about it is an important structuring piece that becomes a valuable measure of whether the teacher is implementing the received professional development and whether the administrators are monitoring the required implementation of the professional development. Remember: What gets monitored, gets done.

What to Bring While Performing Most Walk-Throughs

Before going on a walk-through, it is important to know what tools to bring along to make the assistant principal more effective. There are several items that should come along on most walk-throughs. These include (a) the scope and sequence of the grade and content being visited (this document should represent the state standards), (b) the most current copy of the school's master schedule with the inclusion schedule on it (special education, limited English proficient), (c) an observation form depending on the type of observation or walk being done, and (d) the updated Bloom's taxonomy chart.

The scope and sequence (sometimes called a curriculum guide) of the grade and content where a walk-through is performed is necessary for a variety of reasons. It is rare to find an administrator who is an expert in every content area for every grade in the building. A scope and sequence helps administrators know what is supposed to be happen instructionally in the classrooms being visited.

Administrators can become more knowledgeable about what should be going on instructionally in any grade-level content area by referring to the scope and sequence of the grade and content being observed. Depending on the district, the scope and sequence of what is supposed to be taught each 6- or 9-week grading period can be either one that is produced by the district or one created by teachers following the state's instructional standards.

As mentioned previously, an assistant principal should sit in the planning sessions as teachers decide what they are going to teach according to the standards and what strategies they will use to get the concepts across to their students. Recognizing that it is not always feasible to sit in on all planning sessions due to bus/lunch duty, parent conferences, and so on, it is highly recommended to use the scope and sequence of the grade and content being visited. Teacher lesson plans can also be used, but they should be checked for accuracy to make sure that they reflect what the district's scope and sequence says should be taught at this time.

The pacing of the scope and sequence is significant. It helps ensure that all the standards are taught to students before the end-of-year assessment. It is hard for students to do well on any assessment if the complete set of standards does not get taught.

Another reason to use the scope and sequence is that many times it contains rigorous, engaging activities through which a concept can be delivered or taught. Unfortunately, there is a tendency by some teachers to ignore the engaging activities and instead deliver the information in a more mundane way. For example, it is not unusual to go into a language arts class and see students putting spelling or vocabulary words in alphabetical order or writing them five times each. This can be seen even in some secondary schools, when, in fact, that was not the intended instructional activity written on the scope and sequence but one at a higher level of rigor.

In actuality, there are far more engaging ways to teach vocabulary. Another example can be found in many social studies classes. Students are asked to look up vocabulary terms in the back of their textbooks and write the definitions on a sheet of paper. Research is pretty clear that both these examples are lacking in not only rigor and engagement but effectiveness as well.

Appendix A lists several activities that can help students learn necessary vocabulary in a much more student-centered manner. The Frayer model, for example, is a strategy that works in every content area for struggling readers and special populations, such as limited English proficient and special education. More specific directions on how to use this model, along with several other examples of rigorous, engaging vocabulary strategies, can also be found in appendix A.

To recap this section, it is imperative that an administrator go into the classroom armed with the content knowledge of what instructional standards are supposed to be addressed during that time according to the scope and sequence, using a checklist or document that allows for effective feedback for the teacher when it is not being followed.

Another tool necessary for walk-throughs is a copy of the school's master schedule, which helps the administrator know where each teacher is at any given time and what he or she will be teaching. This is especially necessary on large campuses or those at the secondary level. As part of the master schedule, the special education inclusion schedule should be available for those campuses that have incorporated inclusion teachers. In observing a classroom, the presence of the inclusion teacher should be noted on the checklist form.

Also, note whether the inclusion teacher is sitting or up and moving from student to student, helping anyone who needs it. Due to confidentiality issues, an inclusion teacher (or special education teaching assistant) should never be seen just helping the special education students. The teacher should be available to any student who does not seem to understand the information currently being taught. An inclusion teacher should also plan with the general education teachers whom he or she is serving so that differentiated instruction opportunities can be carried out.

For example, after planning with Ms. Hernandez during the last PLC, Mr. Jones, the inclusion teacher, will take the last 15 minutes of class today and pull a group of students who, according to recent formative data, have not mastered an important concept taught last week. That group will comprise not only special education students but also mainstream and English-language learner students, if they also did not get the concept being reviewed.

The third tool that an administrator must use when visiting classrooms is an observation form. Any observation form used should reflect the school's instructional initiatives as stated in the yearly campus improvement plan.

This form is a key piece to help an administrator document the wonderful or not-so-wonderful activities going on in classrooms. This observation form is crucial to the discussion between the administrator and the visited teacher on what was seen during the observation. It can help a teacher grow by, first, bringing attention to an unsuccessful instructional habit, such as not calling on all students, using low-level questioning, and so forth. It can also become part of the documentation used to help teachers who are reluctant to possibly choose a different career. Appendix G contains a sample of a filled-out classroom walk-through form titled "Campus Best Practices Implementation Checklist."

In this form, it is clear that this school has five areas that it claims to be important enough to monitor. In Section 1, "Clear Expectations," the campus says that it wants its students to clearly know what standard or objective they are supposed to be learning each day. This means that the administrator, when visiting a classroom, looks for whether (a) the objective or standard written on the board, (b) the objective or standard is fully written on the board as opposed to just the abbreviated term (e.g., "Obj. 3.1a"), (c) the objective or standard is written on the board in student-friendly language (many times the formal language used by the state is incomprehensible to students), (d) there are artifacts posted around the room (e.g., criteria charts, rubrics, rigorous student work, projects), (e) the artifacts are recently done (within the last 4 to 6 weeks), and (f) the classroom is a print-rich environment that helps students understand the current concept being taught.

Section 2, "Classroom Visit," asks the administrator to identify what type of walk-through is being done. It also asks the administrator to ascertain whether a portfolio of student work is kept for each student and if the students are filling out profiles after each formative assessment. This particular campus asks that students manage their own learning by filling out the profiles with reflections and goal setting.

The administrator using this form would look for current work in the portfolios and whether the students filled out a profile the last time they were assessed. How thoroughly the student profiles are filled out is also documented. Many times, students rush through filling out the profiles. They turn them in not completely filled out, or they use vague, nonmeasurable language, such as "I will study more," when asked how they will meet their new assessment goals. When this is seen, it is documented on the form and is part of the feedback to the teacher. (For more information on student profiling and profiles, see chapter 5, on assessment literacy.)

Section 3, "Student Participation/Engagement," asks the administrator to look for how thoroughly the students are engaged in what they are learning. Is at least 90% of the class participating and engaged? Is the teacher calling on a student and allowing a wait time that lets him or her process the answer before answering? Or is the teacher just calling out questions and allowing the few "eager beaver" students to answer, letting others off the hook because there is a culture of not all students being called on in that classroom?

If the students are doing independent work or group work, is the teacher monitoring by walking around the room, looking for those who need help, or is he or she sitting at the desk? Is the teacher asking high-level processing questions? For more information on what constitutes high-level questioning, begin with the well-known Bloom's taxonomy. For an updated taxonomy chart that compares the old version to the newer one, see appendix B. Note the change from nouns to verbs to describe the different levels of the taxonomy.

The updated Bloom's taxonomy, which is also a tool that should be included in the administrator's clipboard when doing walk-throughs, reflects the relevance to 21st-century work and can help an administrator listen for key words as teachers question students about a concept. Table 4.1 is a

Table 4.1. Updated Bloom's Taxonomy

Remembering: Can the student recall or remember the information?	define, duplicate, list, memorize, recall, repeat, reproduce, state
Understanding: Can the student explain ideas or concepts?	classify, describe, discuss, explain, identify, locate, recognize, report, select, translate, paraphrase
Applying: Can the student use the information in a new way?	choose, demonstrate, dramatize, employ, illustrate, interpret, operate, schedule, sketch, solve, use, write
Analyzing: Can the student distinguish between the different parts?	appraise, compare, contrast, criticize, differentiate, discriminate, distinguish, examine, experiment, question, test
Evaluating: Can the student justify a stand or decision?	appraise, argue, defend, judge, select, support, value, evaluate
Creating: Can the student create new product or point of view?	assemble, construct, create, design, develop, formulate, write

representation of the new verbiage associated with the long-familiar Bloom's taxonomy.

Administrators listen for question stems that begin with "Defend the position that . . ." or "How does the cell of a cat compare to one in a rose?" or "How did your point of view change after reading/hearing this new information?" Activities such as creating Venn diagrams to compare one thing to another or asking students to judge other students' work through a rubric is very high level and increases student thinking, especially when used often. The updated Bloom's taxonomy found in appendix B would be an excellent short professional development in an upcoming PLC.

For additional ideas on high-level instructional strategies, the book *Classroom Instruction That Works*, by Robert Marzano, Debra Pickering, and Jane Pollock (2003), can be shared in a campuswide book study. The book shows the success of nine instructional strategies gathered from thousands of studies. The research in this book indicates not only what strategies work but also which are the most successful, in descending order:

1. Identifying similarities and differences
2. Summarizing and note taking
3. Reinforcing effort and providing recognition
4. Homework and practice
5. Nonlinguistic representations
6. Cooperative learning
7. Setting objectives and providing feedback
8. Generating and testing hypotheses
9. Cues, questions, and advance organizers (p. 7)

Classroom Instruction That Works makes a wonderful book study for teachers and administrators. During the study, administrators and teachers can select together what strategy should be used with their upcoming standards for which they are planning. Then, as teachers implement the strategies, administrators visit classrooms and observe, giving relevant feedback that leads to teacher growth.

Section 4, "Student Work," of the Campus Best Practices Implementation Checklist, asks the administrator to look for student work posted on the walls in the classroom. It is an effective strategy to have student work posted around the room, but in today's world, the administrator should check to see if (a) the student work is rigorous (meaning, did the activity ask the students to analyze the concept at a deep level?), (b) the work is comprehension level only, and (c) the work is current (within the last 4 to 6 weeks). Not seeing any or all of these components should lead to feedback with the teacher, requesting that he or she post current rigorous student work on the walls.

An FYI on posting student work: Years ago, only work with "100%" written proudly on it was found on the walls. For some students, that rigorous criterion might mean getting through 13 years of school with never once seeing their work posted up on a classroom wall. A suggested recommendation—and this would make a good PLC discussion—is this: Have a bulletin board in the classroom with the title "Look How Much I've Grown!" On it would be posted work, with grades written on the backside, not the front, of those students who have shown effort in their learning. Students who have never had their work posted would finally be rewarded for their effort. "Keep improving!" can be written on the front of these types of papers.

Section 5, "Professional Learning Communities (PLC documentation)," helps administrators record two areas. One is what is happening in a PLC as he or she takes part in it. Are teachers using the time to analyze data, plan lessons collaboratively, write common assessments, receive professional development, analyze student work for rigor and relevance, or see which students need pyramid response to intervention as shown by the data? Or are they spending too much time on operational issues, such as discipline and parents' concerns? These are certainly significant issues but ones that should be discussed during departmental meetings, not PLCs.

The second area that this section documents is the checking of both the PLC binder and a teacher's instructional binder. The PLC binder, as mentioned in chapter 3, is where each content area maintains its agendas, sign-in documentation, meeting notes, articles, and other materials that the department chair and administrators have brought to study and discuss. A teacher's instructional binder would contain lesson plans, scope and sequence, Bloom's taxonomy chart, student intervention lists, parent contact log, and so forth.

Evidence of special education and limited English proficient updates are also included on the checklist and should be looked for in both the PLC binder at grade level and the teacher binder by classroom or period. Special education individual education plans should not be found in the teacher binder, because those must be in a locked cabinet, but special education accommodations and modifications could have a section in the binder due to the importance of having that information. This would also be needed if the teacher has English-language learners. The teacher should have what language proficiency level the students are and whether they are exempt from the state test this year.

Most important, each binder should contain lists of struggling students, ongoing interventions, and the outcomes of the interventions. For more information on the successful implementation of interventions, a study of response to intervention is essential by teachers and building administrators. This should be a beginning-of-the-year review every fall.

Missing or incomplete sections should be immediately addressed by the administrator. Both binders should be checked weekly, especially once the school year is past its first 6- or 9-week period. This is when the interventions should start showing up for struggling students and student profiling should be checked for as well.

The Campus Best Practices Implementation Checklist allows an administrator to have a clear picture of what is happening in the classroom or PLC during the time spent there. Spending 5 minutes every few days in the same classrooms using this type of form allows an adminstrator to have (a) an opportunity to provide constructive feedback to teachers, (b) documentable evidence to help determine if a teacher needs additional support due to patterns of lack of instructional effectiveness, and (c) documentable evidence to help determine if a teacher has benefited from the provided professional development (i.e., is implementing the professional develoment recently provided by the campus or district). It also documents whether a PLC is being effectively managed by the content area's assigned teacher leader.

If a struggling teacher is indeed on a growth plan, two copies of the filled-out form should be given to the teacher. The teacher should sign that he or she received each one, to cut down on the "I never got feedback" complaint. It is never a good idea to place filled-out observation forms in a teacher's box. That can become a confidentiality issue.

To reinforce an earlier concept, it is necessary for administrators, when at all possible, to attend the professional development that the teachers are receiving.

This is a tremendous help when observing in classrooms. Remember the saying "You cannot support what you don't know."

Going Into the Classrooms: Effective Feedback

Once an administrator has set a goal of how many classrooms to observe each week, has printed copies of the scope and sequences for those classrooms, and has gathered other needed items, it is time to go into the classrooms.

Look first at what standard or objective is written on the board, and compare it to what the scope and sequence says should be taught during this period. Is it written in student-friendly language? Do not forget to make a note of what time you went into the classroom and what time you left. Also, was the inclusion teacher present? Was that person walking around helping all students?

Next, notice the students' engagement level. Write on the form whether the students are working in small groups, what level of instructional dialogue is being used, and whether most students (90%–95%) are engaged or participating. Is the teacher doing all the talking, or is the instruction student led? If the students are doing a worksheet, is it a high-level rigorous one, causing the student to process deeply? Can the students answer questions about what they are learning? Is there student work posted? Is the only work posted reflecting perfect work?

After walking around getting a feel for what is happening in the classroom overall, sit down right there and write what you heard and saw before you forget it. Pending an emergency, do not leave until you finish your note taking, especially if going into multiple classrooms. Look for positives as well as opportunities for growth. A sample of a filled-out checklist is also provided in appendix G.

The administrator in this case complimented the teacher for some good practices, such as the grading rubric, performance charts, and having rigorous student work posted. He noted that the students were in small groups discussing the math scavenger hunt and the teacher was monitoring.

The administrator then asked about a group of struggling students, who did not seem to understand the assignment, and wondered how the students had been selected for each group. If the teacher had randomly placed students in groups, then discussing the issue—that is, making sure that each group had a strong student to take the lead in it—might be a more effective way of forming the groups the next time that this type of activity is attempted. That the students had profiled the latest assessment was also noted. Many administrators encourage teachers to answer the posed questions by e-mail or in other written form when face-to-face feedback is not possible in a timely manner.

Helping teachers grow through ongoing, timely feedback is every administrator's job. It may take several weeks of this type of back-and-forth between teachers and administrators before the campus is comfortable with this type of observation, especially if it is not accustomed to frequent visits.

Setting a goal for how many classroom walk-throughs will be done each week is an important part of becoming more instructionally literate. As an administrator frequents classrooms, he or she will learn what effective instruction looks like, who is in need of support through extra professional development and mentoring, and what students need from teachers to help them "get it." When administrators visit classrooms regularly, instructional capacity is built in them as well.

Administrators should set a walk-through goal for visiting a minimal amount of classrooms a week and then work at not letting the campus's busy work keep him or her from reaching the weekly goal. Start with at least 10 classrooms a week. If there are only a handful of teachers being supervised by one administrator, then they should be visited at least once a week, and he or she can visit other teachers as well. Even though those teachers may be supervised by other administrators, it is always good to have another set of eyes check if one administrator is seeing the same thing as the other. This can lead to wonderful instructionally based professional dialogue between administrators. The learning never ends.

CHAPTER 5

~

Step 5:
Get Assessment Literate

Our aim should be to change our cultural practices so that students and teachers look to assessment as a source of insight and help instead of an occasion for meting out rewards and punishments.

—Lorrie Shepard (2000)

As mentioned in the introduction, the current American accountability system has two sides: federal and state. The federal accountability system looks for "adequate yearly progress," otherwise known as AYP. (Currently, legislation driving the federal regulations comes from NCLB, but by publishing date this may have changed, as mentioned in chapter 1.) What the state side of the house does is to interpret through state legislatures what those federal policies will look like in local districts in those states. All of this translates into an accountability that is assessment driven, since both accountability systems require performance data as evidence of student success.

Many assistant principals have gone through a career of being on a campus and have never really had to get involved in testing. The assistant principals who have had operational duties more than any other type of responsibility have been shielded from having to know about assessment, why we give it, what we do with the results, and, more important, how to use them so that they lead to a change of instruction.

Assessments can make teachers more effective. Unfortunately, the "how to do this" has not been rolled out on many campuses. It is human nature to avoid what we do not understand or what we must change; therefore, many administrators are not well versed in assessment literacy. As stated by Newfields (2006),

> often, the biggest challenge in promoting assessment literacy seems to be convincing end-users that the topic is actually worth learning: when many people encounter the arcane jargon and complex statistical formulas sometimes used in assessment, a frequent response is numbness.

Many veteran teachers and administrators have the "didn't have to do it before, not doing it now" attitude. But, without fail, educators become more effective in their work when they look over their test results as soon as they are released or scored so that they lead to an understanding of what instructional strategies were successful and which were not. Those same educators are even more successful at increasing student achievement over time when they learn to look at test results and group struggling students so that an intervention can be started. So doing things the way that they have always been done cannot be an acceptable practice anymore. This is especially when it comes to assessment literacy.

This chapter defines different types of assessments commonly used in most districts and explains their use and importance. Summative and formative assessments are discussed, along with the need to have data-driven analysis, teacher-made common assessments, and student involvement in the assessment feedback process. The importance of assessment that leads to a change in teacher practice and the possible need for student interventions are shared through response-to-intervention information. Finally, the value and necessity of the teacher planning meetings or PLCs to help manage it all are reviewed.

Over the last 40 years, many initiatives have been proposed in state and local education policies, especially having to do with assessment and school reform. All of this is done, of course, in an effort to increase rigorous standards and ensure accountability. The number of states doing minimum competency testing has increased from a small number in the 1970s to 46 in the 1990s to all in 2002 because of NCLB.

NCLB requires schools that accept federal money (Title I funds) to assess their students at the end of each year starting in 3rd grade and ending in 11th grade. Criterion-referenced assessments meet this requirement. Criterion-referenced tests are high-stakes tests where the results have important implications for a campus and its staff as well as the individual students. Students need to pass the state-mandated test to graduate from high school. Licensure testing, also criterion referenced, must be passed to become a doctor, certified public accountant, or lawyer. However, being high-stakes is not specifically a characteristic of a criterion-referenced test. It is how an educational or governmental agency chooses to use the results of the test that makes a criterion-referenced test "high stakes." More important, this type of test is a summative assessment that allows educators to determine whether students understood the curriculum.

Defining Summative and Formative Assessments

The terms *formative* and *summative* have become better understood by educators in the last few years. In a balanced assessment system, summative and formative assessments are both an integral part of information gathering in a school. To obtain a clear picture of student achievement in schools and classrooms, educators must understand and use both types of assessment.

Summative Assessments

Summative assessments are given periodically to determine at a particular point in time what students know and do not know. Many educators associate summative assessments only with standardized tests, such as state assessments. Summative assessment at the district/classroom level is an accountability measure that is normally used as part of the grading process. Other types of summative tests include end-of-unit or chapter tests, district benchmarks, end-of-course or semester exams, report card grades, state assessments used for state accountability, and scores used for federal accountability (AYP).

Summative assessments are usually given after finishing a concept or after a certain period to measure how well students learned the instruction. Because they occur after instruction every few weeks, months, or once a year, summative assessments can also help evaluate the effectiveness of programs, school improvement goals, alignment of curriculum, or student placement in specific programs. Summative assessments do not provide information at the classroom level, nor do they make instructional adjustments and interventions during the learning process, because they happen so far down the learning path. It takes a formative assessment to accomplish this.

Formative Assessments

Formative assessment is a process used by teachers during classroom instruction. Teachers need quick, direct feedback to adjust ongoing teaching to improve students' achievement of intended instructional outcomes. As stated by assessment researcher and author James Popham (2008),

> formative assessment (FA) is a planned process that involves a series of carefully considered, distinguishable acts on part of teacher and student. Referring to a "formative test" misses the mark. The nature of the test does not make

it formative or summative; it's the use of the test that makes this determination. Classrooms without formative assessment focus just on grades. The more activities in a classroom that are formative, the more the classroom is focused on student learning and improvement in that learning. The expanded use of formative assessment is supported not only by instructional logic but also by the conclusions of well-conceived and skillfully implemented research. (p. 5)

Formative assessments are any data that teachers use to measure standards, where the students are, and where they need to be. Students should take part in this as well. These essential data cause teachers to monitor for content mastery and academic growth. They allow for changes and/or interventions. They provide teachers guidelines, and they are assessment *for* learning, not assessment *of* learning, as seen in the chart by Dr. Anne Davies (Figure 5.1).

Anecdotal and informal formative assessment should be the daily bread of any teacher's repertoire. Teachers need to be constantly observing students to know how to modify their lessons, both immediately and in the future. Informal assessment opportunities include teachers (a) observing students

Assessment *of* Learning (Summative)	Assessment *for* Learning (Formative)
➤ Checks what has been learned to date.	➤ Checks learning to decide what to do next.
➤ Is designed for those not directly involved in daily learning and teaching.	➤ Is designed to assist teachers and students.
➤ Is presented in a formal report.	➤ Is used in responding to student work and in conversation.
➤ Usually summarizes information into marks, scores or grades.	➤ Usually detailed, specific, and descriptive feedback in words and in relation to criteria that has been set.
➤ Usually compares the student's learning with either other students or the 'standard' for a grade level.	➤ Usually focused on improvement, compared with the student's 'previous best' and progress toward a standard.
➤ Does not need to involve the student.	➤ Needs to involve the student (the person most able to improve the learning).

Figure 5.1. Assessment *for* learning vs. assessment *of* learning. *Source.* "Assessment for Learning: An Online Resource for Teachers," http://annedavies.com/assessment_for_learning_contact.html.

working independently and in groups, (b) varying the question level according to student ability, (c) monitoring students' products, and (d) sharing concerns and observations with colleagues that lead to a change in instruction. These informal assessments are among some of the "natural" formative assessments that master teachers do, almost without thinking.

Formative assessment can be thought of as "practice" as students learn new information. It helps teachers determine next steps during the learning process, as the instruction prepares students for the upcoming summative assessment. Other examples of formative assessment can include the following:

- Check-for-understanding questions during a lesson.
- Teacher-made tests that assess recent learning, which the students must use after taking the tests to see what they learned versus what they did not learn, as shown by the data.
- Students are given an open-ended question having to do with a recently learned concept and are asked to not only think through their answer but defend or adjust it based on conversations with peers.
- Teacher gives a weekly quiz not only to gain an understanding of who needs to be retaught in what areas but also to share the answers with the students so that they can also be aware of their areas of strength and weakness.
- Students do goal setting along with a reflective log that states what they will do differently (come to tutoring, do homework, pay more attention in class, etc.) to reach the stated goal on an upcoming assessment.
- Teacher shares the item analysis of the latest assessment, at both the classroom level and the individual student level, so that assessment reflection can be done together.

Formative Versus Summative Assessments

Let us pretend that Jonquisha is learning to speak Chinese. Every time that she goes to the lab and practices speaking, she receives a mark off for poorly pronounced or forgotten words. As she continues going to the lab, she gets better over time, and her grades improve. She also begins to learn and write Chinese characters, starting with relevant vocabulary having to do with family, food, and school. She does this by making a vocabulary picture dictionary, adding new characters each week. Her teacher checks her verbal and written skills periodically. Her teacher also redirects her when he sees that Jonquisha is not grasping a certain phonemic concept correctly or is miswriting Chinese characters (formative assessment).

Her final grade for the class is the average of all her grades received while practicing her new language (summative assessment). Because of the initial low grades received during the process of learning to pronounce the language, the final grade would not accurately reflect Jonquisha's current ability to speak Chinese.

This example explains why the traditional grading system needs updating (see Thomas R. Guskey, noted researcher on this topic, for more information, *Practical Solutions For Serious Problems in Standard-Based Grading* [2008]). Would receiving grades on her current ability to speak Chinese tell her what to do differently to improve (*Five Obstacles to Grading Reform* [2011])? What should the summative assessment measure? Should it measure whether she can now speak Chinese at a level appropriate for that class, or should it be the average of all the attempts? This same scenario, when viewed through the lens of formative assessment, would clearly show that the student was improving and should be rewarded in a way to keep her motivated to continue learning Chinese.

This analogy puts into perspective how each type of assessment should be used. Formative assessment should give Jonquisha direction toward what she needs to study to improve, while the summative assessment reflects the measure of what she has learned over time. This same perspective holds true for classroom instruction and student learning.

Effective formative assessments are teacher made (as opposed to paper tests from educational publishing companies), and they assess what students recently learned to see if they "got it." As mentioned previously, it is important that teachers and students review their assessment results, whether they be from an paper-and-pencil test or a project viewed through a rubric, immediately after completion. This allows the student to know what he or she did well and what needs work. It allows the teacher to know where that student is in his or her learning at all times.

Common assessments are a type of formative assessment that is becoming better understood by campus educators. It is called a *common assessment* because a group of teachers have agreed to give the same assessment so that they can come back and discuss the results collectively. They are most effective when they assess what was taught every 2 to 3 weeks. The tests should be constructed carefully, before the instruction is actually taught, keeping the end in mind. Constructing tests before instruction helps keep the teacher focused on the concept as he or she teaches it. Tests do not have to be paper and pencil. They can take the form of other types of agreed-on products or hands-on activities. The results of hands-on activities can be measured through a rubric created by the teachers and shared with the students before proceeding with the activity.

The research bears out that when teachers create the test before teaching the concept, there is less of a chance of deviating from the lesson or missing the instructional timeline before the test is given. Students perform better on assessments created before the concept is taught as well.

By taking the time to create fair, focused, and well-thought-out assessments, teachers can gather evidence and make meaningful judgments about student performance and future instructional plans and decisions. Common assessments should be reviewed by students through reflective practices just like other assessments, to ensure student self-management of learning.

Authentic Assessments

To implement formative assessment to its full effectiveness, students must be involved in the process. Students can both assess their own learning and be a peer resource. As mentioned previously, research shows that involvement in and ownership of their work increases students' motivation to learn. Teachers help students identify learning goals while setting clear criteria for success and providing "authentic assessments" that lead to evidence of student learning. A common definition of authentic assessment asks students to perform real-world tasks that demonstrate meaningful application of essential knowledge and skills. This can take the form of a task for students to perform and a rubric by which their performance is evaluated.

A good example of this is the following. A golf instructor teaches the skills required to perform well and would not assess students' performance by giving them a multiple-choice test. The instructor would put students on the golf course and ask them to demonstrate how well they can swing the club, how far they can hit the ball, and how accurately they can putt into a hole. Although this is obvious with athletic skills, it is also true for academic skills. As mentioned by Jon Mueller on his Authentic Assessment Toolbox website,

> Students can be taught how to *do* math, *do* history and *do* science, not just *know* them. Assessing what our students had learned, we can ask students to perform tasks that "replicate the challenges" faced by those using mathematics, doing history or conducting scientific investigation.

As shown by Figure 5.2, education is moving away from assembly-line skill requirements to needing students to be able to process through to a conclusion, instead of reaching an answer due to having memorized some facts about a concept. Teaching students "soft skills" and not just "hard skills" will

Traditional Assessment	Authentic Assessment
➤ A school's mission is to develop productive citizens.	➤ A school's mission is to develop productive citizens.
➤ To be a productive citizen, an individual must possess a certain body of knowledge and skills.	➤ To be a productive citizen, an individual must be capable of performing meaningful tasks in the real world.
➤ Therefore, schools must teach this body of knowledge and skills.	➤ Therefore, schools must help students become proficient at performing the tasks they will encounter when they graduate.
➤ To determine if it is successful, the school must then test students to see if they acquired the knowledge and skills.	➤ To determine if it is successful, the school must then ask students to perform meaningful tasks that replicate real world challenges to see if students are capable of doing so.

Figure 5.2. Traditional assessment vs. authentic assessment. *Source.* "What Is Authentic Assessment?" http://jonathan.mueller.faculty.noctrl.edu/toolbox/whatisit.htm#similar.

prepare them better for their future world, which will in no way look like the one that most of us came from.

With authentic assessment, assessment drives the curriculum. In the traditional assessment model, the curriculum drives assessment. What form the assessments take can be crucial to totally understanding what a student has learned. Portfolios are a means through which this can be managed.

Portfolios are collections of student work representing a selection of performance tasks. Portfolios in classrooms today originated from the fine arts tradition in which they showcase artists' work. In a school setting, a portfolio may be a folder containing a student's best pieces and the student's evaluation of the strengths and weaknesses of the pieces. It may also contain one or more works in progress that show the creation of a product, such as a report or essay, evolving through various stages of conception, drafting, and revision. A student can use the portfolio to keep ongoing projects and samples of best work judged through a rubric. Teacher and student can conference around the samples in the portfolio, looking for how the student has grown over time. It is also an excellent tool to show parents during conferences. Unfortunately, elementary teachers have embraced the authentic assessment concept more than secondary teachers, although the instructional impact on students at all levels can be tremendous.

Another effective tool that should go into the portfolio is the student profile. Too many times, all over the country, students are assessed, with teachers and sometimes administrators pouring and fretting over the results. The teachers may confer with other teachers over what to do differently and may include administrators in the planning, all the while forgetting the most important player in the game . . . the student.

New research is validating the need to involve students in their own assessment feedback. Called "student self-management of learning" or "self-directed learning," sharing assessment results with students is the best way to increase student interest and internal motivation to increase achievement. A template showing the different components of the student profile is shown in Figure 5.3.

There are several parts to the student profile that make it relevant and worth the time, especially in the beginning, when teachers and students are attempting to go through it together the first few times. The upper third of the profile requires the students to fill in their own "mini-item analysis." Each column represents a different standard, and each row within the standard represents the number of the test item that tested that standard. The students place a Y or N in each cell if that particular test item was passed or not. In the *Mastery* row, the students say how many items they got correct along with the total number of times the standard was tested. So in Figure 5.3, Joey mastered six of six test items tested for summarization but only two test items out of five for inferencing.

It is essential that the students go through this activity in each content area that they are profiling. Not only does this give students an opportunity to see how they did on each standard tested, but it also allows for relevant math practice using decimals and percentages. Done regularly in each content area, students will eventually learn that 3/5 is 60% and will remember that on future math tests, even though they have been practicing it in other content areas.

The middle of the profile asks students to reflect on how they did, using measurable and specific language. It is critical that teachers do not accept profiles from students that have not filled this out or who have made statements that are vague and cannot be measured. For example, "How do you feel you did on this assessment and why?" should be answered similar to what is on Figure 5.3. Answers such as "I did bad" or "I did okay" are not acceptable and are not measurable and specific.

For "What are your goals for this assessment next time you take it?" again, the answer should be well defined. "Do better" is not a goal. For "What will you do differently to improve on the next assessment?" "Study harder" is a

Student Profile

Name of Assessment __3 Week Common Assessment__

(Reading) Math Science Social Studies **Date** _Oct. 15th_
Circle content being profiled

Name _Joey L_ **Grade/Section** 8th **Yr to Date Attendance:** _missed 4 days_ **Pass/Fail 6 weeks?** P

Number of times Standard was tested							
7							
6	15/ Y						
5	18/ Y	20/ N	21/ Y				
4	10/ Y	11/ N	19/ Y		22/ Y		
3	8/ Y	9/ Y	17/ Y		16/ Y		
2	5/ Y	4/ Y	13/ N	14/ Y	7/ N		
1	3/ Y	1/ N	12/ N	2/ N	6/ Y		
Mastery:	6/6 100%	2/5 40%	3/5 60%	1/2 50%	3/4 75%	15/22	
Standard # and Name:	**8.2c** Summarization	**8.3b** Inferencing	**8.4a** Main Idea	**8.6a** Context Clues	**8.6b** Comprehension	**Total 68%**	

How do you feel you did on this assessment and why? Be specific!

I did well in summarization and okay on comprehension, but I need to work on inferencing, main idea, and context clues.

What is/are your goal(s) for this assessment next time you take it?

I want to keep getting high scores in summarization and comprehension, and get inferencing, main idea, and context clues up to at least 75% next time I test on those.

List what you will do differently to improve on the next assessment (Be specific!):

I will come to Saturday School and tutoring after school. Also, I will be better about getting to class on time and not having anymore absences.

Create a bar graph using the data from above:

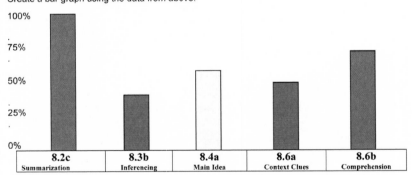

Student Signature: **Parent Signature:**

Figure 5.3.   Sample student profile.

frequent and easy phrase that students want to put down but is really meaningless, since the student has not written what that looks like as far as future behaviors and actions are concerned. The answer such as the one in Figure 5.3 is closer to what students should write.

The last third of the student profile gives another relevant math opportunity. Many students struggle with graphing, so asking students to graph their results adds an additional chance to reinforce its context within a meaningful activity. Bar graphs can be replaced by asking the students to use line graphs instead, after the teacher has seen that the students have mastered bar graphing.

Finally, asking the student to sign the profile before turning it in turns it into a character-building document. If Joey wrote that he would attend tutorials and Saturday school but did not, then the teacher can ask Joey questions such as "Joey, you signed your name to this document that you would come to Saturday school and tutoring, but I never saw you once last week at either one. Are you not a man of your word?" This is a time for Joey to take personal responsibility for doing what he signed he was going to do.

The parent signature is there so that when there is a parent conference, a parent can sign that he or she saw it and that it was discussed. It is not a good idea to send profiles home, since not all of them come back. It is safer to leave them in the portfolios until such time that a parent comes to school for a meeting or conference.

For more information on the use of the student profiles and for additional templates, please see http://www.askdrbgood.com.

Alternative Assessments

Due to the issues surrounding the limitations of traditional testing, interest in alternative assessments has become more prominent. Assessments that spotlight critical thinking skills and a more authentic way of assessing student performance and achievement are being used more consistently. Alternative assessments can include performance assessments, oral presentations, demonstrations, exhibitions, short-answer questions, essays, and portfolios. These changes in assessments have affected content standards that are embedded in core curriculums at a national level. A good example would be the standards for the National Council of Teachers of Mathematics, which now calls for more authentic assessment of all learners.

A chapter on assessment cannot only be about assessment; it must be tied to curriculum, best practices, and so on. This is being stressed because all these layers work together. Just as states, districts, and schools must work toward the same goals, so must the "written, taught, and tested curriculum" all work together to affect student learning.

Assessing Culturally Diverse Learners and Special Populations

With the passage of NCLB—and with the increasing emphasis on account-ability testing in general—the need to produce valid and fair assessments for all students has become a matter of pressing national concern. Along with the growing numbers of English-language learners (ELLs) in the United States comes a need for not only an efficient means of assessing such a cultur-ally and linguistically diverse population but a fair one as well.

There is also a need to understand the effects of the students' native language on psychological assessment results. Many issues have come up about cross-cultural testing. These include assessment validity, the use of inappropriate norms, ethnocentrism and cultural or ethnorelativism, cultural stereotypes and prejudice, acculturation, and language barriers. On top of that, there has not been much material focusing on assessment of bilingual students. Assessment of bilingual students raises questions specific to lan-guage use. For example, the assessment of fully bilingual and partly bilingual students may show different decisions about what language to use and how to interpret results.

Let's review for a minute the research on language learning. Mark La Celle-Peterson and Charlene Rivera (1994) state that

> even though minimal survival skills in English can be achieved fairly quickly, the ability to use English for academic purposes—that is, school success skills in Eng-lish—takes longer to develop. While ELLs can and do learn in accordance with high academic standards, their accomplishments will likely be under-estimated if they are assessed in the same way as their monolingual peers. (p. 2)

They further argue that "assessment systems must be designed to help all students—not just monolingual learners—meet the educational goals set by and for them, and help educators monitor the effectiveness of educational programs in enabling all students to reach those goals."

Historically, when compared with their native English-speaking peers, ELLs consistently demonstrate lower academic achievements. National data have indicated that in English reading, 76% of third-grade ELLs performed below grade level and in mathematics, 54% performed below grade level.

A long-standing issue that has been the concern of special and general educators in the past several decades is the disproportionate representation of culturally and linguistically minority students in special education programs. ELLs were 27% more likely to be placed in special education in the elementary grades and almost twice as likely to be placed in special education in secondary grades. Again, culturally appropriate context is hypothesized as the key to effective instruction and intervention for culturally and linguistically diverse students and children.

According to Abedi and Gándara (2006), "English language learners now are the fastest growing subgroup in the nation" (quoting Kindler, 2002). Consequently, fairness and validity issues relating to their assessment must be among the top priorities of the national education agenda. ELLs have historically lagged behind their English-proficient peers in all content areas, particularly academic subjects that are high in English-language demand.

The literature suggests that this performance gap is explained by many factors, including parent education level and poverty, the challenge of second-language acquisition, and a host of inequitable schooling conditions in addition to measurement tools that are ill-equipped to assess students' skills and abilities. ELLs are more likely to be taught by teachers without appropriate teaching credentials and with little classroom experience than other students. A recent study of 4,800 teachers of ELLs in California, who responded to a survey about the challenges they faced in teaching ELLs in their classrooms, found large percentages of these teachers expressing the concern that they were not prepared to teach these students.

To help reduce language factor effects in the assessment of ELLs, testing accommodations have been suggested and used in both local and national large-scale assessments (see appendix C). Accommodations are provided for ELLs in an attempt to "level the playing field" and measure their content knowledge as fairly and accurately as possible. In a 2001 policy brief, the National Center for Research on Evaluation, Standards, and Student Testing provided the findings regarding testing accommodations for ELLs (listed in Table 5.1).

Some accommodations are more effective than others. Providing extra time, a glossary of key terms on the test *plus* extra time, or reducing the language complexity of the test questions resulted in substantially higher test scores for ELLs and non-ELLs. Providing a glossary without extra time did not increase ELLs' performance, possibly due to information overload.

Other special populations, including special education students, have assessment requirements that must be carefully followed. Individualized educational plans for these students contain what their learning goals are, what test they will take, and what accommodations or modifications they must have. In addition, supplemental educational aides may be called for. All of these are also monitoring pieces for administrators. Each administrator over a

Table 5.1. Policy Brief Regarding Testing Accommodations for English-Language Learners (ELLs)

Findings

Translating test items from English to a student's native language does not significantly improve ELL performance when the language of instruction is not the student's native language.

The only accommodation that narrowed the gap between ELL and non-ELL students was linguistic modification of those test questions with excessive language demands.

In addition to language proficiency, other background factors influence ELL performance. These factors include length of time in the United States, overall grades, and student mobility.

Source. National Center for Research on Evaluation, Standards, and Student Testing (Abedi, 2001).

content area should confer regularly with the inclusion teachers to make sure that they are following their inclusion schedule, tutoring, meeting the individualized educational plan goals for their students, and meeting regularly with the mainstream teachers to plan how to meet the needs of the special education students each week.

The takeaway here for administrators is to make sure to seek out the state and district policy on testing ELLs, special education, and other populations. Discuss this with the ELL and special education department chairs at the campus to become more educated in this important area. The special education subgroup and the ELL subgroup count toward AYP each year if they are in sufficient numbers on a campus. This is an excellent exercise in preparation for the principalship.

Balancing Assessments

As teachers gather information and data about student learning, several categories may be included. To better understand student learning, teachers need to consider information about the products (paper or otherwise) that students create and the tests they take, observational notes, and reflections on the communication that occurs between teacher and student or among students. When a comprehensive assessment program at the classroom level balances formative and summative student learning and achievement information, a clear picture emerges of where a student is relative to learning targets and standards. Students should also be able to articulate this shared information about their own learning. Student-led conferences, a formative assessment strategy, are a valid method of viewing that picture. The more that is known about individual students as they engage in the learning process, the better the teacher can adjust instruction to ensure that all students continue to achieve by moving forward in their learning.

Tying It All Together: The Written, Taught, and Tested Curriculum

In this age of accountability, we must focus attention on not only what is taught but also how it is tested. There a need for reliable assessments aligned to rigorous curriculum and how to use the information provided by the assessments. A process must be in place to help campuses understand how to read data and turn the information into an action plan. As Learning Point Associates (2000) pointed out,

> when this process is absent, confusion reigns. Staff from many schools indicated that they did not see the connection among teacher-administered in-class assessments, their norm-referenced district test, and the large-scale state assessment. Nor did they know what to do with this information.

Administrators need to recognize that it is imperative to understand the practices that work best, tying together the written, taught, and tested curriculum. Current research literature has assembled assessment literacy, reflective practices, professional development, and student interventions into a four-component process. These components take into account assessing students, collaboratively reflecting over data, professional dialogue, interventions for students based on data results, and reassessing to measure the impact of the changes made in both teacher practice and student interventions. What does this look like for a campus? How does one tie in the four components so that they are executed properly and regularly? As mentioned previously, PLCs have been one of the mechanisms used to achieve this through encouraging teachers to discuss data and share strategies in an effective manner. Others, besides Rick DuFour (2004), the originator of the practice, began to favor the use of PLCs. Eastwood and Lewis, as early as 1992, recognized that

> learning communities are the means by which we can break [teacher] . . . isolation and foster a collaborative environment and reflective culture. In fact, creating a collaborative environment has been described as "the single most important factor" for successful school improvement initiatives and the "first order of business" for those seeking to enhance the effectiveness of their school. (p. 215)

A group of administrators and teachers analyze data and come to two conclusions. One has to do with "What did the students learn?" and the other one, "How well did the teacher teach this?" When teachers share their data in a collaborative setting such as a PLC meeting and begin asking questions based on the data, professional development begins to happen. Listen for these types of questions: "Who taught this standard better than me?" "How did you teach this?" "What strategy did you use to get this concept across?" "Can I come watch you teach this?" "Your special education students did better than mine! How did you teach this concept so they were able to achieve better scores than my students?"

When the word *data* is used, it does not only mean performance results. Formative data that can and should be brought to the PLC to be professionally discussed include student projects, group work, student work, students' graphic organizers, and teachers' observations. Looking at this type of "common assessment" gives teachers the opportunity to see which teacher has been able to pull more rigor out of his or her students, as shown by student work.

Response to Intervention

Assistant principals need to know about student interventions or what needs to be done when a student has not learned. The current response is called *response to intervention* (RtI) as a way of reaching learners when the data show that they have not learned. This subject can take up volumes, so although it will be touched on here, wise assistant principals will research it more thoroughly and bring it to the campus if RtI is not there already.

As mentioned by the RtI Action Network (2010),

> the need for Response to Intervention or RtI can be made quite clear when information on the "why" of RtI is presented, along with information on the impact this model has on student performance. The following are the typical areas where information is provided in support of the need to change to an RtI approach:
>
> 1. The adequate yearly progress (AYP) requirements of No Child Left Behind and state departments of education.
> 2. The inclusion of RtI in the regulations for the implementation of the Individuals with Disabilities Education Improvement Act of 2004.
> 3. The research evidence that supports the positive impact of RTI on student performance, particularly in reducing disproportionality (over-representation) and improving the academic and behavioral performance of students.
> 4. The positive effects of having a consistent model and procedures that are used to make educational decisions for all students.

Professors Martha J. Coutinho and Donald P. Oswald (2004) state that RtI is a multitiered intervention model that involves all students and teachers rather than only students who are at risk for a disability. It provides intensive early intervention for students who do show signs of learning difficulties before they are referred for a comprehensive special education evaluation. This model could also reduce the disproportionate representation of culturally and linguistically diverse students in special education. For example, ELLs who are struggling in reading would be given more assistance and support in reading instead of being referred to special education. Ongoing progress monitoring would show the effectiveness of the interventions.

Theoretically, this sounds logical, but in reality there are many factors that could affect how students respond or whether they would respond at all. How this model can best serve ELLs remains unknown. But in spite of the little-known empirical evidence supporting RtI's use with ELLs, the promising goal of RtI is to ensure that quality instruction, good teaching practices, differentiated instruction, and intervention opportunities are available at all settings for all struggling students. These settings should include general education, special education, and any other specialized instruction to meet the individual needs of students with or without disabilities. An important takeaway is that the main goal of RtI is not to identify specific learning disabilities; rather, data from RtI will help identify students who indeed need special education and related services due to a specific learning disability because the series of early interventions have not been shown to work.

Another term for RtI is *pyramid RtI*. It is the same concept but in a more graphic or visual form. A graphic example of a pyramid RtI is included in appendix E.

Practices for an Assessment-Literate Campus

An assessment-literate campus includes the following best practices monitored by campus administrators:

- Have all pertinent staff able to access all necessary data across the district and programs on the district's data management system to enable up-to-the-minute analysis of data, including statewide assessment results, language proficiency data, and formative assessments.
- Have a monitoring system in place to ensure that strategies, modifications, and assistive technology are being properly implemented in every classroom.

- Provide effective modifications, learning style accommodations, assistive technology in daily instruction, curriculum-based assessments, benchmark testing, and statewide assessment.
- Include students in the review of assessment data by reviewing the test's item analysis with them, having students profile their weak standards on a regular basis so they can see growth, and having students do goal-setting toward the next assessment.
- Consider and document intensive remedial instruction and prescriptive tutorials as shown by frequent diagnostic data.
- Stress instruction-driven assessment, individual decisions for each student and each curricular area, appropriate justifications for assessment decisions, consideration of least restrictive environment testing, and use of modifications and high expectations.
- Use data effectively to drive instruction and assessment (RtI/pyramid RtI models).
- Implement inclusion and coteaching strategies for teachers of special education and English as a second language.
- Use a student support team committee with a pyramid RtI or RtI model to provide monitored effective research-based best practices and prescriptive strategies and interventions.
- Use admission, review, and dismissal and ELL committee decision-making process to ensure that instructional settings, language placement, assessment decisions, and support services are appropriate and that students are making progress in their learning goals.
- Start the use of accommodations and instructional aides for ELLs and special education students early in the school year.
- Discern core curriculum problems from teacher instructional problems through the ongoing use of PLCs.

The content departments, in conjunction with bilingual, ESL, special education, elective, and fine arts teachers, should

- Review and examine data and current practices to identify areas that were not sufficiently addressed or that require greater accountability.
- Provide decisions with specific course of action to eliminate gaps and provide prompt, corrective action.
- Request input from other program partners and external resources.

All campus staff members should be involved with high-quality professional development for

- Understanding the need and use of curricula and assessment measures.
- Using assessment and evaluation results to guide instruction and provide necessary early instructional strategies.
- Implementing and accelerating effective instructional strategies that are engaging, rigorous, and relevant along with culturally responsive instruction and student-driven active learning.
- Implementing RtI.

This chapter introduces or reinforces assessment literacy components that will lead assistant principals who are working toward the principalship to understand the connections among the written, taught, and tested curriculum. The campus leader can no longer just be a manager. That person must be an engaged instructional leader who understands the need for assessment and how to use it to help teachers and students be more effective in their roles. By becoming more assessment literate before reaching the top spot, an ambitious assistant principal will be able to not only "walk the talk" but also accurately "talk the walk" in career-changing future interviews (practical testing tips for the campus are provided in appendix F).

CHAPTER 6

~

Step 6:
Organize Yourself! Become
More Internally Disciplined

Many people struggle with organization; it is a difficult task. Often, life's obstacles can be so overwhelming and so overbearing that we do not know what to do with them all. If something is not done to organize it all, it becomes one great big mess, especially when combining the professional and personal parts of our lives.

During the first half of this book, assistant principals learned about the importance of becoming more instructional and not to just go through the day tending to the three b's (books, butts, and buses). This chapter is about helping busy assistant principals become more internally disciplined to follow their new goals. The difference between winners and losers is follow-through. Nine times out of 10, an academically successful campus is a winner because its administrators regularly monitor the implementation of the campus's goals and initiatives. This takes internal discipline and organizational skills that must be learned. Without these developing skills, some assistant principals may not earn the principalship.

In this chapter, steps are discussed that will help organize busy administrators. A weekly organizational template illustrates how even busy high school assistant principals can organize themselves right into the classroom, when they previously thought it impossible. Let's look at practical ways of becoming successful in daily routine and organizational skills.

Many times, busy administrators look at others who are in the same position and wonder how it is they are able to accomplish so much more during the same period of time. They often write off organizational skills because they are "too busy." The truth is, being organized is not so difficult when a routine or a schedule is written down. Follow the steps in this chapter, and becoming organized in the professional and personal setting is suddenly possible.

Action 1: Organize Your Space

Make an appointment to spend an hour of "clean up my space at work" time. It can be done by either staying an hour after the normal workday or coming in an hour early. Write this day and time on the calendar and honor it. It may not be at the same time each week, but make sure that it is built it into the weekly calendar.

Start by clearing the desk, then move to bookshelves, chairs, and even floor if necessary. Look through what is piled there, and get rid of it if it is not used often (or put it in storage). Take home those personal effects that do not need to be in the office, and be generous when it comes to throwing things away. Keep those atta-boy or atta-girl possessions that are only absolutely necessary. Give everything a designated space, especially for items used on a frequent basis.

Sort through the papers, stacking those that require actions in one pile, those that need to be filed in another, documents that must be shredded in the third pile, and throw away what is no longer needed. Ask yourself, "Do I really need this? Will I need this in a year's time? Should I be the one keeping this, or does this fall under someone else's watch? Is there someone out there who could use this? Will I really miss this if I do not have it?"

Put discipline documents in one location, instructional in another, and so on. Have a specified location for documents or forms needed on a frequent basis. This may sound obvious, but to no surprise by most, busy administrators do not tend to take the time to get organized but will complain how hard it is to find needed documents in their office. "The desk monster ate it" is not going to be acceptable when a principal asks for important papers that were last known to be in the possession of the assistant principal.

This first activity is important. When it is inconvenient to get or find things, then organization skills are more likely to fail. Make it easy to get to what is used daily, and make sure that the habit of putting things away in their newly organized spot is followed.

Many administrators need to know what "organized" looks and feels like. An organized space is simple to use, as there is enough room for each item to be placed in a convenient location. Every item in the office has a correct place. Get in the habit of spending that once-a-week hour to "put back" the office to its previous organized manner.

Why go to this effort? When parents, students, and teachers go into an office that is organized, it makes them feel calm, open, and welcomed. An organized office provides a good first impression, especially when critical conversations may be needed. And let's face it . . . "If we look good, we must be good" is often the case. A disorganized assistant principal is never a good choice for the top spot.

Action 2: Put It Back

Whatever is removed from its rightful place, when done—put it back! Once everything has an established spot, keep it that way. The need to get into the habit of putting things back as soon as you are finished using them is the next crucial part. Do not place documents, forms, folders, or any paperwork on the desk, shelves, or windowsill and think, "I'll put it back or file it later." That is playing a mind game that you will rarely win. Put it away then. Most administrators carry rings with many keys and other door openers. Always place them in the same location, along with your cell phone and radio, when walking into the office. Do the same with the stapler, scissors, staple remover, and so on. Do it until it becomes an unconscious act. Always putting things in their designated place will save a busy administrator's sanity in the long run.

Action 3: Plan With a Calendar

Put the calendar in a place where it can be perused each morning; on the wall near the desk, on the computer desktop screen, or flat on the desk are easily accessible places. Wherever it is, make sure that it is part of the daily routine. Be meticulous about updating it with meetings, trainings, parent/ student conferences, and school events, as soon as they become apparent. Many tech-oriented assistant principals now use their cell phones that are synched to their computer calendar instead of a paper calendar. This is fine. The important piece is to post new calendar events immediately upon learning of them and then get in the habit of synching the phone to the computer once a day. Oftentimes, an effective assistant principal becomes the go-to person for a busy or disorganized principal, who relies on this assistant principal for accurate dates and upcoming events.

Upon arriving into the office each morning, review the daily and weekly tasks and appointments. Make it a habit. Daily and weekly goals for classroom walk-throughs are much more attainable for administrators whose daily routines involve their calendars. Administrators who habitually use their calendars are less likely to miss important meetings. Assistant principals will not get into the principal's seat, nor should they, if they cannot or do not learn to accurately keep and follow a calendar. For further affirmations as to the use of calendar planning, see Figure 6.1.

Action 4: Use a Weekly Planner

Planners are especially valuable for administrators who have a multitude of commitments, such as visiting several classrooms each day, sitting in PLCs, and meeting with teachers, students, and parents. Most administrators have so many daily appointments and a variety of daily duties that they have trouble keeping track of their schedules. A weekly template should be a natural part of an administrator's routine. Either late Friday afternoon or early Monday morning, ambitious assistant principals plan out their week based on the commitments logged on a main calendar.

As shown by the planner in Figure 6.2, the assistant principal can write in known tasks, duties, meetings, trainings, and so forth every day. A copy of this weekly planner can be given to the principal, office manager, secretary, or school receptionist as a way of being able either to find the assistant principal or to explain to parents why the assistant principal cannot come to the office right now. An effective assistant principal will make a copy of this planner with all the weekly duties/tasks that remain the same each week and just fill in new appointments that appear on the calendar.

Part of becoming more organized is to help campus personnel also learn to honor certain times that you are not available, unless it is an emergency. With principal permission, it should be rare for an assistant principal to be pulled away from the time spent with classroom visits. Office personnel can be trained to explain to parents that the assistant principal would be happy to meet with the parent at a designated time and then make the appointment.

When a campus moves in this direction, it is not long before parents understand that "this is how we do things at this school." A principal must take the time to explain to parents during site-based meetings, Parent–Teacher Association/Parent–Teacher Organization meetings, and other parent opportunity meetings early each year about the importance of administrators being able to go into classrooms frequently along with completing other job duties. Dropping everything to meet with anyone who asks, at any given time, does not make for an organized campus. Most parents are more than understanding about this and soon learn to ask for appointments instead of demanding immediate service.

For 10 Minutes each Week

Organize Yourself from the Monthly Calendar to Weekly Planner so that it will help you be:

Dependable:
the principal can count on you to be where you are supposed to be

Successful:
the classroom walk-thru goals are met

Committed:
the teachers appreciate that you take part in PLCs

Punctual:
you attend meetings on time

Dedicated:
you honor instructional as well as operational duties

Figure 6.1.   The use of calendar planning.

School Name: _Sunshine Elementary_   **Calendar for Week:** _10/2 - 10/7_   **Admin. Name:** _Ms. Joy_

Monday	Tuesday	Wednesday	Thursday	Friday	Sat.
7:30 – 7:55 Calendar\To Do list	*7:30 – 7:55 Calendar\To Do list*	*7:30 – 7:55 Calendar\To Do list*	*7:30 – 7:55 Calendar\To Do list*	*7:30 – 7:55 Calendar\To Do list*	Sat.
Before School	Before School	Before School	Before School	Before School	School
Duty Station: 8 – 8:30 a.m.	Duty Station: 8 – 8:30 a.m.	Duty Station: 8 – 8:30 a.m.	Duty Station: 8 – 8:30 a.m.	Duty Station: 8 – 8:30 a.m.	Y N
Buses	*Buses*	*Buses*	*Buses*	*Buses*	
Period 1- 8:30 – 9:25 a.m. *Tardy passes/Walk hallways*	Period 1- 8:30 – 9:25 a.m. *Tardy passes/Walk hallways*	Period 1- 8:30 – 9:25 a.m. *Tardy passes/ 9 a.m meeting With Joe's mother*	Period 1- 8:30 – 9:25 a.m. *Tardy passes/Walk hallways*	Period 1- 8:30 – 9:25 a.m. *Tardy passes/ 9 a.m. Parent meeting*	**Notes:** *My turn this Saturday, unlock doors 8 a.m.*
Period 2- 9:25 – 10:20 a.m. *Classroom visits*	Period 2- 9:25 – 10:20 a.m. *Classroom visits*	Period 2- 9:25 – 10:20 a.m. *Administrator meeting*	Period 2- 9:25 –10:20 a.m. *Classroom visits*	Period 2- 9:25 – 10:20 a.m. *Classroom visits*	*Organize office today.*
Period 3- 10:25 – 11:20 a.m. *Classroom visits* *11 a.m. lunch duty*	Period 3- 10:25 – 11:20 a.m. *Classroom visits* *11 a.m. lunch duty*	Period 3- 10:25 – 11:20 a.m. *Classroom visits* *11 a.m. lunch duty*	Period 3- 10:25 – 11:20 a.m. *Classroom visits* *11 a.m. lunch duty*	Period 3- 10:25 – 11:20 a.m. *Classroom visits* *11 a.m. lunch duty*	
Period 4- 11:25 – 12:20 p.m. *lunch duty*	Period 4- 11:25 – 12:20 p.m. *lunch duty*	Period 4- 11:25 – 12:20 p.m. *lunch duty*	Period 4- 11:25 – 12:20 p.m. *lunch duty*	Period 4- 11:25 – 12:20 p.m. *lunch duty*	
Period 5- 12:25 – 1:20 p.m. *Meeting w/ parent volunteers*	Period 5- 12:25 – 1:20 p.m. *Bookroom duties*	Period 5- 12:25 – 1:20 p.m. *Cover class for Ms. Jones*	Period 5- 12:25 – 1:20 p.m. *Classroom visits*	Period 5- 12:25 – 1:20 p.m. *Conf. w/ Maria Eliso- finish discipline log*	
Period 6- 1:25 – 2:20 p.m. *Classroom visits*	Period 6- 1:25 – 2:20 p.m. *Bookroom duties*	Period 6- 1:25 – 2:20 p.m. *Classroom visits*	Period 6- 1:25 – 2:20 p.m. *Discipline log/parent calls*	Period 6- 1:25 – 2:20 p.m. *Classroom visits*	
Period 7- 2:25 – 3:15 p.m. *Cover for Mr. Longel*	Period 7- 2:25 – 3:15 p.m. *Discipline log/parent calls*	Period 7- 2:25 – 3:15 p.m. *Prepare for after school training*	Period 7- 2:25 – 3:15 p.m. *Classroom visits*	Period 7- 2:25 – 3:15 p.m. *Walk hallways, make presence known*	
After Sch Duty Station: *In front of building*	After Sch Duty Station: *In front of building*	After Sch Duty Station: *In front of building*	After Sch Duty Station: *In front of building*	After Sch Duty Station: *In front of building*	

Figure 6.2. Sample weekly planner.

Blank templates of weekly planners are provided in appendix D for both elementary and secondary levels or for schools that have seven periods and those that have block schedules. Times for activities such as PLCs, walk-throughs, and other weekly meetings (e.g., the weekly administrative meeting with the principal) should be built into the weekly planner. Be sure to also schedule time for (a) making calls to parents about students (both positive and negative), (b) completing operational activities such as weekly bookroom checks, (c) dealing with referrals from teachers regarding unruly students, (d) listing games and other after school activities that require supervision, and, most important, (e) updating the weekly planner.

Action 5: Multitask

Perform multiple tasks at the same time or combine activities when possible. For example, when walking back to the office to meet a parent, walk into a classroom or two along the way. Even going into a classroom for 60 to 90 seconds will remind the teachers and students that administrators are close by and interested in what is happening instructionally. The parents will not notice a 2-minute delay, and the administrator will have added more information to what is known about those teachers. Asking the parent to wait 60 seconds more while you write observations and reminders is not a bad idea, either. Parents will remember only that you were gracious while you met with them, not that it took an extra 3 minutes to get to their matter.

Remember to carry the classroom walk-through forms at all times because writing what was observed, even for that short period, can be important down the road. Short trips into classrooms, done frequently over a several-week period, allow assistant principals to notice positive and not-so-positive instructional trends that can be corrected sooner instead of later. Toward the end of the school year, when it is time for formal evaluations, having many classroom observations on the teachers to be evaluated gives a much richer evaluation, especially if the administrator has had several conferences with teachers whose observations indicated that they were struggling instructionally or with classroom management.

Other combination activities might include the following:

- An administrator can ask a student who needs "a talking to" to come to the bookroom for the discussion, to simultaneously deal with the student during the weekly bookroom check time. Walking back to the office to chat with the student wastes precious time, especially in light of the fact that it is almost impossible for an administrator in a busy school to get from one side of the building to the other without another interruption.

- When the call comes on the radio from a monitor requesting the presence of the assistant principal, ask the monitor if that is something that he or she can handle for the time being while you finish doing your walk-throughs. Many times the security officers or monitors react by immediately asking for an administrator, when, in fact, they can be trained to handle most of the work involved in the more serious offenses. Then the assistant principal can receive the paperwork and the information and make the call to parents after the walk-through time is finished. This, of course, should be done on a discretionary basis, with common sense prevailing. Possible criminal violations should be expedited as quickly as possible.

Take care of the little things where and when one can, always streamlining steps whenever possible. It is the way to juggle the many duties resting on an assistant principal's shoulders.

Action 6: Make To-Do Lists

Write down your daily tasks on an easy point-by-point tick-off system. Each morning, check the weekly planner for the day's highlights and list the "must-dos" for the day. Prioritize them and commit to making sure that they are done. As stated in Step 4, an ambitious assistant principal will sit down either late Friday or early Monday morning and plan out the week based on the commitments from the main calendar to make sure that nothing is missed. Keep a small pocket-sized notepad in the breast pocket or purse, and check on the completion of the daily "must-dos." Do not trust memory. The hectic pace of today's schools is such that memories cannot be relied on. Mental notes are not worth the paper they are written on.

Try to write everything down. Take copious notes in meetings. Circle or highlight items in the notes that need to be added to the main calendar, along with any item that requires action to be taken (i.e., "action items"). Make it a habit to add these action items to the main calendar before going home each day. Over time, an assistant principal will become the "go-to" person as far as keeping the campus on track. That can only mean good things for that future campus principal.

Action 7: Delegate Responsibilities

As often as possible, delegate different responsibilities to people in your school. This may mean using teachers, parent volunteers, or students, depending on the task, since it is rare that an assistant principal has his or her own administrative assistant. Before tapping into the other available people and resources on your campus, make sure to have principal permission to delegate a task to the person. Be sure that the persons chosen have the necessary tools to complete the task satisfactorily. Just because there are willing folks does not mean that they are up to the task. Ask the principal for permission to use a school clerk or teaching assistant for an hour each week to help with filing student records. But remember: Teacher growth plans and discipline records would be best filed by the administrator, due to confidentiality issues.

Student office helpers and parent volunteers can help in the bookroom, organize and help keep teacher workrooms clean, help with lunch and recess duties, and so forth. Having more hands and eyes increases a campus's chances of staying organized and safer as a whole. Anytime that there is a plethora of volunteers helping keep a campus in order, positive public relations is also occurring. Those same volunteers are the first ones to say wonderful things about what is going on at the school while out in the community. They are the people that can correct misconceptions or myths about "what's going on" at the campus. This is especially important at the secondary level, where parent involvement is oftentimes not as high.

Make sure to follow up on the completion of the delegated task to make sure that it was done correctly. This means adding that action step to the calendar. This is often a forgotten step yet the most important one. As mentioned previously, monitoring is the step that will ensure that the request or task gets done. Assuming that the delegated task is done is a dangerous habit. Successful administrators do not assume much of anything anymore.

An important final reminder for this step is this: Confidential material is *never* to be available to the people who should not see it. School offices are full of confidential data. Discipline records, performance data, and social security numbers are easily found in many administrator offices. This is a tremendous confidentiality concern and must be safeguarded against. Parents, volunteers, and students can help with many tasks but never any that involve discipline or performance data at the teacher or student level.

Assistant principals become more internally disciplined by making sure that they complete the tasks that they set out to do. There is no point in writing a to-do list if there is no plan to stick to it. Do not procrastinate. Remove all distractions and get what needs to be done, *done!* A checklist is included in Figure 6.3 so that it can be posted as a reminder until the steps become a habit. Post it near the calendar so that it is within easy visual reach.

Although it takes time and effort to become more internally disciplined, the payoff makes it worth it. An internally disciplined assistant principal becomes more professionally and personally satisfied with his or her lifestyle. Others also notice and admire those traits when they see them in that administrator. Principals are selected from pools of organized and ambitious assistant principals. Those assistant principals who show that they are managing instructional and operational tasks successfully will be among the first selected.

Hey, Busy Future Principal:

Have You Done This Yet This Week?

🔲 **Step One: Organize Your Space**

🔲 **Step Two: Put it Back!**

🔲 **Step Three: Plan with a Calendar**

🔲 **Step Four: Use a Weekly Planner**

🔲 **Step Five: Multi-task**

🔲 **Step Six: Make To-Do Lists**

🔲 **Step Seven: Delegate Responsibilities**

Figure 6.3.   Seven-step checklist for aspiring principals.

CHAPTER 7

∽

Step 7:
Embrace Instructional Technology

Instructional technology is here to stay! The 21st-century principal must be a master of technology . . . that is to say, not necessarily a master of how to use instructional technology so much as why one should and how to go about building capacity in sometimes reluctant teachers (and other administrators).

The principal must also encourage teachers to embrace instructional technology. A strong principal role models what he or she wants from others in the building. But administrators cannot wait until they become a principal to become more instruction technology literate; they must assume the principalship already having embraced it as an assistant principal.

This chapter defines instructional technology, including information on why our 21st-century learners must have technology as part of their instructional day and how technology affects learning for both teachers and students. As written by Gilbert Valdez, PhD, director of North Central Regional Technology in Education Consortium (2010) and codirector of North Central Eisenhower Mathematics and Science Consortium:

Teaching is changing and, in many ways, becoming a more difficult job because of increasingly numerous contradictory expectations, including the following:

- We are living in an age of information overload with the expectation that students will learn high-level skills such as how to access, evaluate, analyze, and synthesize vast quantities of information. At the same time, teachers are evaluated by their ability to have students pass tests that often give no value to these abilities.

- Teachers are expected to teach students to solve complex problems that require knowledge necessary across many subject areas even as they are held accountable for the teaching and learning of isolated skills and information.
- Teachers are expected to meet the needs of all students and move them toward fulfillment of their individual potential even as they are pressured to prepare students for maximum performance on high-stakes assessment tests that are the primary way to measure performance and instructional ability.

Dr. Valdez mentions that technology can help meet some of these expectations and make teachers—and their students—more successful. However, the world is now changing at a yearly rate instead of over generations, due to the rapid advancements being made in technology. As mentioned previously, educational needs must shift from teaching and learning isolated skills and information within each content area to teaching skills that enable students to solve complex problems across many areas. Dr. Valdez is clear that "educators must prepare for a technology-rich future and keep up with change by adopting effective strategies that infuse lessons with appropriate technologies."

The chapter on assessment literacy (step 5) discussed the need for authentic assessment. Instructional technology makes authentic assessment needs even more important: Assessments must keep pace with effective instructional technology use. All this while educators at every level—teachers especially—actively pursue professional development that enables a lifelong exploration of ways to enhance the teaching and learning by embedding relevant instructional technology into the curriculum.

There are resources and lesson plan samples that show how including instructional technology into the everyday curriculum enriches the learning for students today. But more than anything, the importance of technology is shared by bringing the research of futurists such as Mark Prensky and Ian Jukes. By the end of this chapter, even the most unwilling of readers may be ready to dip his or her toe into the instructional technology waters, finally understanding how needed and safe the waters can be!

Marc Prensky (2001) is an internationally acclaimed speaker, writer, consultant, futurist, visionary, and inventor in the critical areas of education and learning. He has researched, studied, and written about the positive impact that gaming can have on children. Prensky is amazed over all the debate about the failure of education in the United States. His contention is that the nation has ignored the most fundamental of its reasons. He states very dramatically that our students have changed completely. The students that we have in our schools today are not the people that our educational system was intended to teach. He writes,

> Today's students have not just changed *incrementally* from those of the past, nor simply changed their slang, clothes, body adornments, or styles, as has happened between generations previously. A really big *discontinuity* has taken place. One might even call it a "singularity"—an event which changes things so fundamentally that there is absolutely no going back. This so-called "singularity" is the arrival and rapid dissemination of digital technology in the last decades of the 20th century.
>
> Today's students—K through college—represent the first generations to grow up with this new technology. They have spent their entire lives surrounded by and using computers, videogames, digital music players, video cams, cell phones, and all the other toys and tools of the digital age. Today's average college grads have spent less than 5,000 hours of their lives reading, but over 10,000 hours playing video games (not to mention 20,000 hours watching TV). Computer games, email, the Internet, cell phones, and instant messaging are integral parts of their lives.
>
> It is now clear that as a result of this ubiquitous environment and the sheer volume of their interaction with it, today's students *think and process information fundamentally differently* from their predecessors. These differences go far further and deeper than most educators suspect or realize. "Different kinds of experiences lead to different brain structures," says Dr. Bruce D. Perry of Baylor College of Medicine. . . . It is very likely that *our students' brains have physically changed*—and are different from ours—as a result of how they grew up. But whether or not this is *literally* true, we can say with certainty that their *thinking patterns* have changed.

So here is one important reason why administrators must embrace technology: Today's students have been changed by the technology with which they have grown up. Prensky continues:

> What should we call these "new" students of today? Some refer to them as the N-[for Net]-gen or D-[for digital]-gen. But the most useful designation I have found for them is *Digital Natives*. Our students today are all "native speakers" of the digital language of computers, video games, and the Internet.
>
> So what does that make the rest of us? Those who were not born into the digital world but have, at some later point in our lives, become fascinated by and adopted many or most aspects of the new technology are, and always will be compared to them, *Digital Immigrants*.
>
> The importance of the distinction is this: As Digital Immigrants learn—like all immigrants, some better than others—to adapt to their environment, they always retain, to some degree, their "accent," that is, their foot in the past. The "digital immigrant accent" can be seen in such things as turning to the

Internet for information second rather than first, or in reading the manual for a program rather than assuming that the program itself will teach us to use it. Today's older folk were "socialized" differently from their kids, and are now in the process of learning a new language. And a language learned later in life, scientists tell us, goes into a different part of the brain.

Those of us who are Digital Immigrants can, and should, laugh at ourselves and our "accent." But this is not just a joke. It's very serious, because the single biggest problem facing education today is that *our Digital Immigrant instructors, who speak an outdated language (that of the pre-digital age), are struggling to teach a population that speaks an entirely new language.*

This is obvious to the Digital Natives—school often feels pretty much as if we've brought in a population of heavily accented, unintelligible foreigners to lecture them. They often can't understand what the Immigrants are saying. What does "dial" a number mean, anyway?

Prensky forces all Digital Immigrants to understand the seriousness of choosing not to become part of the technology that is being made available on a more common basis in our schools. If the adults in a building are choosing not to embrace instructional technology, they are choosing to not teach the way that our Digital Natives need it, and that can no longer be an acceptable practice. If professional development in this area is not occurring, immediate measures must be taken to start the transition from traditional teaching to enriched learning with the aid of technology.

Ian Jukes (2006), an educator researcher, read what futurists were predicting in terms of world trends 20 to 30 years ago and then checked to see if their predictions came true. Jukes agrees wholeheartedly with Prensky and takes it a bit further. He calls digital natives "screenagers" who see the computer screen as something to "manipulate and interact with," not to be a passive audience with, like the television watchers of old and digital immigrants. He further states why educators must come around to understanding this new student:

> How do we know this? A great deal of brain research, in what is called the neurosciences, has been undertaken in the past few years. This research is validating much of what we suspected from the psychological research, particularly the psychological sciences. The bottom line is that children today are FUNDAMENTALLY different from previous generations in the way they think, in the way they access, absorb, interpret, process and use information and above all, in the way they view, interact and communicate in and with the modern world. And this holds profound implications for us both personally as parents and professionally as educators. (p. 3)

As mentioned by Jukes, the way that 21st-century students process and interpret information has huge implications as far as how they learn and how we need to facilitate their learning. Every day that digital immigrants ignore this, our digital natives slip further and further away from us to where they can get the information they need and want in the manner to which they have become accustomed. On a serious educational note, how many of our current and past dropouts could possibly be a result of our not recognizing their "digital" thinking and learning needs?

Instructional technology is just what it sounds like: using computers, CD-ROMs, interactive media, modems, satellites, teleconferencing, podcasts, webcasts, webinars, and other technological means to support learning. There are now lesson plans on how to incorporate cell phones, MP3 players, iPods, iPhones, virtual worlds such as Second Life, Facebook, netbooks, and other "student-friendly" technologies into the everyday curriculum. All that is needed is the encouragement by tech-friendly administrators and teachers to incorporate them in a relevant and meaningful way into today's classrooms.

Let's discuss some instructional technology facts. The National Center for Education Statistics (2007) reports,

> In fall 2005, nearly 100 percent of public schools in the United States had access to the Internet, compared with 35 percent in 1994. In 2005, no differences in school Internet access were observed by any school characteristics, which is consistent with data reported previously. Public schools have made consistent progress in expanding Internet access in instructional rooms. In 2005, 94 percent of public school instructional rooms had Internet access, compared with 3 percent in 1994. Across school characteristics, the proportion of instructional rooms with Internet access ranged from 88 to 98 percent. Ratio of public school students to instructional computers with Internet access went from 12.1 students per computers in 1998 to 3.8 students per computers in 2005.

As stated by this compelling research, instructional technology must be embraced by aspiring future principals, not ignored. This is never going to go away. It will continue to grow in its potential to affect classrooms and teachers. It has already conquered our children; now we must get on board with it as well.

How Instructional Technology Affects Learning

Written Curriculum

Instructional technology, used in a relevant and consistent manner, has the potential to significantly expand the breadth and depth of a teacher's everyday curriculum. Using the Internet, students can access information far beyond that of the traditional textbook. Technology can be used to individualize and adapt to students' specific learning styles. It has the power to enhance overall knowledge accumulation, putting the focus on the processing and interpreting of information that leads to new conclusions, not just content mastery.

For teachers, instructional technology means having a curriculum that is on an online platform. It can be accessed either at work or at home, any hour of the day. The online curriculum contains links to other research and resources with which to enrich the lessons. It means having a data management system where current and longitudinal student and teacher assessment data are housed. It is having information about a student at one's fingertips at any hour of the day for immediate instructional instruction or intervention. These data can be shared with students and parents during each student or parent conference. If one is out of instructional or intervention ideas, go to the Internet and blogs to find an answer.

For administrators, the instructional technology opportunities abound as well. Along with monitoring the use of the online curriculum and data-management systems by teachers, administrators can now look at lesson plans online, check teacher data by class or period, and keep records and documents in online folders instead of piled on the desk. The possibilities are endless and habit forming. Out of campus discipline ideas? Go to the Internet and blogs to find an answer.

Taught Curriculum

Instructional technology significantly affects the role of teachers, since it changes their role from expert to facilitator or coach. The structure of schools and classrooms changes through use of instructional technology because teachers who are knowledgeable in the use of instructional technology do not want rows of desks; they want open spaces for group work, areas for students to be able to discuss what they have found online that leads them to new conclusions. These discussions could take place on beanbag chairs instead of desks. Plus, instruction is no longer limited to the school building or classroom. Students can take courses or supplement learning from global satellite feeds or the Internet. Learning can take place at home, at school, or anywhere else that has the capacity for a smartphone, which can access the Internet, a laptop, or a computer. But these scenarios speak of classrooms and teaching and learning to come. Unfortunately, too few schools and districts are ready to emulate any of these models.

Tested Curriculum

As instructional technology develops and becomes more affordable for all districts, the computer infrastructure increases. Students will have the ability to complete yearly state assessments online. The implications of this are profound. Teaches and students can receive immediate feedback regarding student performance. They do not have to wait several months until everyone gathers in the fall at the opening of the next year before realizing how well teachers taught and students learned.

Immediate results help teachers focus more on building feedback loops directly into the learning process rather than having to wait until the assessment has "cooled off" in the eyes of the test takers as well as the test administrators. Summer professional development will be more relevant and meaningful if it can be based on information learned before school was out.

With instructional technology, students can obtain frequent and accurate feedback, make corrections to their work, and structure learning experiences around their individual needs. They can keep portfolios online of their assessments, organized by learning standard, so that they know their weak and strong areas. They can reflect in their online journals as to why they are performing instructionally as they are and what they will do differently to change that. They can also set a goal, and once they have tested again and the results are placed on that profile, the computer can show the students in different graphs, how they did, and whether they met their goal. Plus, it can be ongoing and cumulative, so as they get stronger in a standard, it would be indicated by a continuous graph indicating past and current performances for each learning standard. This would become instructionally relevant for the students as far as using data and graphs in a meaningful way is concerned.

Instructional Technology Devices

Instructional technology devices vary as much as the way that they are used in classrooms. Computers and laptops are now a staple in most classrooms. SMART boards have replaced the blackboard in many classrooms across the country. SMART boards hook up to a laptop or computer and an InFocus projector. The projector sends the information from the computer, which can then be manipulated directly on the SMART board as if it were a blackboard and computer in one. Lesson plans for these boards can be found easily with Internet search engines by searching "lesson plans using a SMART board" for all grades and content areas.

Another device found in many classrooms is the "clicker." These devices, which mimic a remote control, alter classroom dynamics, engaging students with the power of feedback. Clickers give students the opportunity to solve the answer in their heads or on a small whiteboard, then click the correct answer, usually a multiple-choice option. Because students answer anonymously, clickers help ease fears of giving a wrong answer in front of peers or expressing unpopular opinions. The teacher can then see immediately what percentage of students got the problem correct and can do a reteach right then.

Researching online should be a common occurrence by now. With librarians or *media specialists*, as they are called in the 21st century, as ready facilitators of online research, teachers can team with them to plan upcoming projects together.

Video games are also found in many of today's classrooms, often used as review or reteach opportunities for students. There is much out there as far as offerings are concerned, so it would behoove a wise assistant principal to help teachers sensibly select video games and programs and then monitor the implementation of these selections.

Devices and software applications abound that can deepen and enrich a content's curriculum. It is how those devices are used that makes them relevant tools that engage students and help them process the required learning standards.

As mentioned earlier, computers are now found in most classrooms. Although this is the norm, many veteran teachers are admittedly not yet comfortable with even simple or basic technology. These teachers need to understand that students use the Internet to research and find information on their homework topics. More often than not, students use the Internet to find facts, which they then, if not carefully monitored, cut and paste onto a document and turn in as their completed work. Lessons on plagiarism are now a necessary part of the classroom instructional technology world.

The opportunity to go online and research teacher-led topics should involve looking for resources that help answer a high-level question posed about the concept being studied. As mentioned by the updated Bloom's taxonomy (appendix B), students should be analyzing (appraise, compare, contrast, criticize, differentiate, discriminate, distinguish, examine, experiment, question, test) or evaluating (appraise, argue, defend, judge, select, support, value, evaluate) and not just using lower-level Bloom's, which is remembering (define, duplicate, list, memorize, recall, repeat, reproduce, state). Using today's tech tools can lead to lower-level skill use just like textbooks of old, unless monitored by savvy administrators.

A good example that I have seen myself is this: A high school social studies class had student-made posters pasted all around the room. Although they were very nicely done, the information on them contained demographic information about China. They all also listed what products were generated by the country and what its gross national product amounts and exports were. Instead of those posters being the final product on a lesson on China, that information might have been better put to use in answering questions such as "Why did China pass a law forbidding each family to have more than one child?" "What impact did this law have on the population of China over time?" "Why do you think it had that impact?" "Has the Chinese government made any changes to the law?" "If it did, why did it change the law?" "If the law hasn't changed, why hasn't it?" "Did this law cause a change to the Chinese culture? Explain." "Do you think the United States needs to pass a law like that? Why or why not?"

Using facts as a foundation to higher-level questions is the only way that information should be used. No more cute "numbers" posters! Assistant principals must monitor for rigor, through relevant, thought-provoking questions. It might take a professional development or two, but using instructional technology to lead to higher-order thinking is a must in the 21st-century school.

Online classrooms are those that involve creating and designing web pages and blogging and tweeting, which is done by using social networks that help students find sources and information that lead to a new or deeper understanding of a concept. It is thought that the traditional classroom setting of desk and chairs may disappear within the next few years and be replaced by wireless "barns."

These barns, or large open-spaced areas, allow students to meet in groups, sit on sofas and comfy chairs, and discuss their assigned project. Students share their information gathered through communication with people who have real knowledge on their assigned topic. They e-mail authors and ask questions or send surveys to groups of people to help come to new conclusions. Students may also use Internet sources, such as podcasts, websites, and video clips.

For example, a group of students is given the task of projecting the impact that 100,000 people will have on their city's roads in the next 20 years. The students have to figure out what is currently being spent on road development, how city managers go about predicting road use decades in advance, what implications there are in terms of gathering the needed funds to build the roads, and how they would be maintained.

Students divide the work so that each member has a particular area to research and bring back to the group in an allotted period. Some students might surf the Internet looking for answers; others might call the city's municipal center to talk to civil engineers in charge of road design and construction; and others might even talk to the city manager and interview him or her for the needed information.

The interest and relevancy factors are obvious with projects like this and can be done as early as upper-level elementary grades. It is not hard to imagine fewer students dropping out of school as the engagement of students through project-based learning increases.

Let's take time to talk about cell phones and the impact that they have on schools today. Cell phones have been banned from schools in the past, although many districts are reversing that because of safety issues, as in what happened at Columbine High School. Many parents insist on sending their child to school with a cell phone, and they want to be able to talk to him or her before and after school. Although the bans have largely been removed, the problems—or distractions—of cell phone technology have only increased.

Cell phones today allow users to do so much more than just a few years ago. They are used not only to call others but also for texting and taking and sending photos and video clips. Cell phone use can be inappropriate and undesirable on middle and high school campuses when not monitored. Cell phones are also minicomputers, allowing users to go online and find immediate answers or needed information on any subject. Most districts have policies that require students to keep cell phones off during school hours, unless an emergency occurs. Unfortunately, these policies are often broken, as students find ways to elude detection by using increasingly more compact cell phones. Some of the problems with cell phone usage by students in schools include the following:

- Sending text messages during class time
- Cheating on tests by sending or receiving answers
- Bullying or harassment through unwanted text messaging
- Receiving and sending sexually inappropriate text messages and photos of students, now called "sexting"
- Filming fights or other negative scenes and posting them online for others to see
- Using and abusing them in locker rooms and restrooms

However, there are definitely positive educational uses for cell phones that, when exploited by technology-wise teachers, increases relevancy and student engagement. As mentioned by Teaching Today, a website hosted by a nationally known textbook publisher (McGraw-Hill, 2010), uses of the cell phone as a teaching tool include the following:

> *Calculators.* Although most schools have them in math class, other classes that do not have them on hand for students can benefit from number crunching. For example, social studies students studying elections can quickly determine percentages of electoral votes or other scenarios. Science classrooms can use them to perform calculations related to fieldwork.
> *Digital cameras.* Not all schools or classrooms are outfitted with digital cameras, although many can benefit from them. For example, students can use them to document a variety of things for multimedia presentations

or reports. Fieldtrips can be documented and incorporated into digital travelogues.

Internet access. Many phones have wireless Internet access, thus opening up a world of possibilities for class use. Science students might conduct fieldwork and submit their observations or data to either an internal or external data gathering site. Students can subscribe to podcasts that are produced or offered by a multitude of other sources.

Dictionaries. Students in literature and language arts classes can benefit from being able to quickly query the definition of a word. Additionally, students who are English learners especially can benefit from translation dictionaries, which are becoming available on cell phones.

Figure 7.1 shows an example of a poster found on the wall of a math class in a secondary school. Cell phones are slowly but surely making their way into schools. I have also seen locations in school cafeterias deemed "Munch & Chat Phone Zone" areas.

The implications of having students carrying cell phones are tremendous for administrators. Acknowledging that a large number of students bring them to school each day should lead to campus policies that can be implemented by school staff. Teachers can help set the tone by explaining to students early in the year the school policies regarding their use, then following through on the consequences should the policies be broken.

Some school now have a "no show, no use" rule. If a student is caught using a cell phone (or even just holding it in some schools), it is taken away by a teacher or administrator and placed in a safe place in the office. It cannot be picked up until the following Friday after paying the district's $15 fine. Many more students comply when this type of rule is in place.

Additional time and ink could be used to share how devices such as MP3 players, iPods, and virtual worlds such as Second Life, netbooks, and so forth can be embedded into the everyday curriculum. Instead, in collaboration with a group of eager teachers, research these tools and then challenge them in actually implementing some of the lessons found through this research activity. It may finally awake the sleeping instructional technology giant in teachers that the students are waiting for.

The important piece to take away from this chapter is that instructional technology is not only here to stay but is a constantly changing, always developing opportunity for positive use by teachers under the watchful eyes of campus administrators. Assistant principals can help guide teachers into the 21st century by modeling the educational uses of available technology and its many devices and by offering professional development on instructional technology that leads to relevant and engaging student work.

In this Classroom,
Food and Drinks
are
Prohibited
and
Cell Phones
Turned Off
Except
for
Time Keepers!!!

Figure 7.1. Sample poster prohibiting cell phone use.

To make sure that a structured plan for instructional technology is in place, Google "ISTE National Educational Technology Standards and Performance Indicators for Administrators" (see Textbox 7.1 for other web resources). Regardless of the technology, experts in the field of education and technology have come together to develop technology standards for administrators and teachers. This has been done at the international level and the state level. These standards and performance indicators for administrators can bring focus to a school's culture of technology. Most campuses have an IT (information technology) person. Make sure that he or she is aware of and using these standards.

Remember: It is not a matter of just exposing teachers to instructional technology information. Campus administrators must also monitor the implementation of the professional development with the expectation that what teachers are trained in makes it into the classroom. It may be that what was learned during a professional development is first discussed during the next PLC. The discussion would center on how the technology will be implemented in their classrooms. Each assistant principal over a content area should talk about how the culture of the school must move to keep up with technology. This must be done not just for the sake of the expense of technology but because it can do so much for the students. Teachers must be led to understand that "it's not just knowing, it's doing" as well. And assistant principals must inspect what they expect!

Textbox 7.1.   Other Helpful Websites

ASCD, http://www.ascd.org/. ASCD (formerly, the Association for Supervision and Curriculum Development) is an educational leadership organization dedicated to advancing best practices and policies for the success of each learner, whether at the adult level or the student level. ASCD Edge allows educators to discuss current educational topics through forums and blogs.

ASCD News Briefs, ascd@smartbrief.com. ASCD News Briefs provides daily information to one's e-mail on educational topics.

CARET, http://caret.iste.org/index.cfm. The Center for Applied Research in Educational Technology has identified an excellent list of resources consisting of annotated URLs, online journals, and article reviews.

Edutopia, http://www.edutopia.org/tech-integration. The George Lucas Foundation has gathered a plethora of resources that can greatly help administrators. Watch videos, read examples, and communicate with others with the focus of research-based strategies that utilize technology to help students.

eSchool News This Week, http://www.eschoolnews.com. eSchool News provides current information on a variety of technologies and how they are influencing education. Besides being able to sign up for the free weekly information, administrators can stay current with upcoming events, informative videos, and relevant resources and webinars.

Technology & Learning Magazine, http://www.techlearning.com. Administrators will find helpful information regarding best practices, contests, webinars, tech forums to answer questions, and resources to support themselves as well as their teachers. Registration is free.

CHAPTER 8

~

Step 8:
Say Tough Things to
Nice People with Grace

Of all of the species on earth, we human beings are the ones who specialize in voluntary mind change: we change the minds of others, we change
our own minds. We have even crafted various technologies that allow us
to extend the sweep of mind change: powerful mechanical artifacts like
writing implements, televisions, and computers. In the coming decade,
mind changing will continue and, in all probability, accelerate.

—Howard Gardner, *Changing Minds* (2004)

Many teachers choose to become administrators because effecting change
in the classroom alone no longer provides enough satisfaction. The need to
affect a whole campus gradually overtakes some to the point where they are
willing to go back to school and get their administrative certificate. These
teacher leaders look anxiously to the future when they too can work first
with a strong principal as an eager assistant principal and then, when deemed
ready by the powers that be, as principal of one's own campus. Unfortunately,
this scenario leaves out many important skills that must be developed by assistant principals before they can assume the principal chair.

We have spent the last seven chapters exploring how to become stronger
instructional leaders and how to find the time to do the operational and
instructional parts of the assistant principal job. However, other skills are essential to have if one is going to be an effective leader and principal. Many of
the practices and strategies offered in the previous chapters involve encouraging teachers to do something either a bit different or very different. Now,

time will be spent discussing how to help reluctant teachers to change so that they become more effective in their instructional practice. Learning how to say tough things to nice people with grace is a skill that leaders must develop because it is a necessary one to effect change among an unwilling staff.

Hard Skills Versus Soft Skills

In the work world, there are different skill sets that help employees handle the everyday business of "work." Literature in the corporate world separates these skill sets into two areas. One is called "hard skills"; the other, "soft skills." Hard skills are identifiable procedures related to an organization's core business. Examples in education include administrating, teaching, computer protocols, safety measures, budget procedures, and testing.

These skills are measurable, specific, and easy to observe and quantify. They can be easy to train, because most of the time the skill sets are brand new to the learner and no unlearning is involved. A teacher is not born a teacher, for example, but develops into one, as that person goes to a "teacher college" or enrolls in a teacher alternative certification program and learns instructional methodologies. As a future teacher, he or she is gradually exposed to the best practices of teaching; then, after a certain amount of time and courses, he or she is allowed to "student teach," thereby putting into practice what was learned through coursework.

Administrators must also be developed from administrator-certified teachers, who learn the operational and instructional parts of the role, such as managing textbooks and discipline while supervising lunchrooms and observing in classrooms. All those skills have measurable evidence that show whether the teacher or administrator is carrying out one's job duties. A teacher can be observed teaching just as an administrator can be observed supervising a cafeteria at lunch or making daily classroom observations.

By contrast, "soft skills," which some call "people skills," are harder to observe, quantify, and measure. People skills are needed for everyday life as much as they are needed for work. As stated by Dennis E. Coates (2006), CEO of Performance Support Systems, Inc., these skills have to do with

> how people relate to each other: communicating, listening, engaging in dialogue, giving feedback, cooperating as a team member, solving problems, contributing in meetings, and resolving conflict. Leaders at all levels rely heavily on people skills, too: setting an example, teambuilding, facilitating meetings, encouraging innovation, solving problems, making decisions, planning, delegating, observing, instructing, coaching, encouraging, and motivating.

It is not hard to find campus leaders who need to take a "Social Skills 101" class over again (and nobody is sure that they took it the first time). That type of leader, one lacking in social skills, rarely has a happy, motivated staff. Assistant principals with principal dreams must look deep and hard at themselves and see what areas they may need to stretch and develop.

School staff come to a campus with interpersonal behavior patterns that are already thoroughly ingrained due to having relied on these behaviors for years. All people learn how to deal with relationships and other life challenges at an early age. They observe how the people (e.g., their parents) around them do things. They experiment, and they stick with what works for them. Everyone ends up with a myriad of people skills unique to him or her, despite having some behaviors that might cause problems with others. By the time that administrators and teachers get to a campus, the way they deal with people has been reinforced for many years.

In the case of an administrator, there are two sides at which to look. One is how to handle one's self when a conflict arises, and the other is how to handle the other person. In other words, how an administrator handles oneself, when he or she must have what may be an uncomfortable conversation, decides how well that conversation is going to go with that person.

One of the skills that an assistant principal must develop before reaching the principal position is to learn to say tough things to nice people with grace. In other words, he or she must be able to talk professionally with another person—usually in this case, a teacher—and tell him or her something that that person may find uncomfortable. It could be anything from asking the teacher to dress more professionally, as stated by district policy, to having to put that teacher on the third growth plan for the year, which may eventually lead to that teacher's termination. As difficult as these conversations are, they are crucial and necessary, especially if a campus is going to be considered "well run."

A well-run campus contains administrators who are quick to praise and quick to redirect, always professionally and always consistently. It is imperative that the staff members of a school feel that the administration is "equitable and fair" as it metes out praise and constructive criticism. Employees like to be able to rely on their supervisors, and they expect them to react in a consistent manner when a coworker "steps out of line." Morale issues arise when administrators are perceived as "unfair" or "having or playing favorites" through their reactive behavior.

An effective principal helps assistant principals develop the soft skill of saying tough things to nice people with grace. The principal uses "people made" issues that pop up on campuses as learning tools. The principal may hold weekly or twice-weekly administrative meetings with the discussion of personnel issues as an agenda item. Consider the following scenario:

- During the weekly administrator meeting, the principal mentions that she has noticed Ms. Jones slipping in late some mornings due to not having a class first period. The principal assigns Ted, the new assistant principal, to discuss this with Ms. Jones. She reminds him to take copies of the teacher's sign-in roster, to show where the teacher has either failed to sign in or signed in late, and a copy of the district's attendance policy. She also asks him to copy her on the follow-up e-mail noting the discussion points that Ted shared with Ms. Jones during their meeting.
- During the next administrator meeting, the principal thanks Ted for a job well done. She states that the follow-up e-mail sent to Ms. Jones contained excellent, professionally presented points from their discussion. She also says that she has noticed Ms. Jones arriving to school on time since the meeting about her attendance.

Two important things happen when a principal follows through with handling discipline in a timely manner. First, the staff members, who have also noticed that Ms. Jones was coming in late, now see that she arrives on time. They assume, knowing the principal as they do, that the teacher has been "talked to." They know that this type of behavior is not tolerated, and they like that it is dealt with quickly and fairly.

Others do not push the envelope, so to speak, because they know that they too will be dealt with in a similar fashion. There is comfort in that for staff members. Employees of any organization appreciate knowing that they are able to rely on their leader to deal with those employees who step out of line in a quick, consistent, fair, professional manner.

The second thing that happens is that the soft skills of assistant principals begin to develop. As the principal delegates these opportunities for "crucial conversations" with oversight, practicing soft skills become a natural behavior for assistant principals. Very few people come into an administrative job with these skills well developed. Most new or emerging leaders need to work on gaining stronger people skills, so it is important that future principals begin working on this area as assistant principals.

If, by chance, the opportunity to practice saying tough things to nice people is not presented to the assistant principal, it can still happen. The assistant principal simply has to become the driver of this procedure instead. An assistant principal who is willing to develop this set of skills can do the following:

- Ask to meet with the principal.
- If the principal is currently handling all the staff "redirection," ask if some of that can be delegated to the assistant principals as a way of helping develop the skill of saying tough things to nice people with grace.
- Suggest a course of action. That is, outline each step of the process with the principal, including meeting notes, follow-up e-mail, and outcomes.

Most principals are happy to have someone else to shoulder the responsibility of helping with staff "redirection." This can often be an area that falls off a busy principal's radar due to the daily catastrophes that so often derail well-intentioned administrators. Many teachers and other staff members have been allowed to continue inappropriate behavior because the school administrators did not have enough documentation to enable the employee to "grow or go."

Once approval has been granted from the principal to assist dealing with staff issues, knowing how to help people change their minds is important. Howard Gardner, a Harvard professor well known for his "multiple intelligences" research, has written about understanding the approach to take to attempt changing peoples' minds. Research tells how people resist change, to the point of only one out of nine will change the way that he or she lives, even if it involves a life-or-death health situation, such as heart disease (Deutschmann, 2007).

Even after making a change, people have a tendency to revert to their old behaviors, a process called *homeostasis*. So understanding how to help people change their minds and lead them to healthier work habits is an important skill to learn for any administrator. Gardner (2004) mentions that there are seven "levers" to help change peoples' minds and habits:

1. Reason: When we are trying to persuade others, reason plays a pivotal role—especially among those who consider themselves educated. Most businesses rely on analysis and logical processes when making decisions. The rational approach involves identifying relevant factors, weighing each in turn, and making an overall assessment.
2. Research: The scientific approach collects relevant data and analyzes it in a systematic manner (often statistical) to verify or cast doubt on promising trends. Research needn't be as formal as this, however. It may entail identifying events and forming judgments as to whether they warrant a change of mind.
3. Resonance: While reason and research appeal to the cognitive aspects of the mind, *resonance* applies to our emotions. Appealing to one's feelings and creating emotional resonance are among the more powerful means of

changing minds. Resonance is often achieved after one hears reason and research arguments, but it may occur on an unconscious level. As a relationship of trust or connection to the mind-changer develops, one is persuaded to change.

4. Representational Redescriptions: This term describes what happens when a change of mind becomes convincing in several different ways that reinforce each other. For example, a PowerPoint presentation may present the same concept using percentages, bar graphs, and other graphic images, all of which explain the same key concept in distinct ways.

5. Resources and Rewards: So far, the possibilities for mind-changing lay within reach of any individual whose mind is open. It is sometimes more likely to occur when resources are available. In psychological terms, this is known as *positive reinforcement*. Ultimately, however, unless the new course of thought is congruent with the other criteria—reason, resonance, and research—it is unlikely to last beyond the provision of rewards.

6. Real-World Events: Wars, terrorists, natural disasters, and economic depressions can influence mind-changing. On the positive side, so can prosperity and peace. It is easier to convince a nation to go to war after a terrorist attack, even when the facts are lacking.

7. Resistances: The six factors involved in changing minds have thus far been positive. It is unrealistic to assume that you won't encounter resistance—the strong force that negatively affects mind change. In our early years of life, we change our minds frequently to develop, learn, and become competent. Research demonstrates that changing minds becomes more difficult with age. We develop strong views and perspectives that are resistant to change.

Gardner reminds us that when the first six factors work together, it increases the chance that people change their minds. Of course, it is also easier to change peoples' minds when they are not strongly resistant against what is being asked. The power of resistance must be taken into account; ultimately, it is what makes changing a mind almost impossible to occur quickly.

At the campus level, these levers can be applied at the individual level or with a group of people. Here is a scenario involving one person:

Ms. Gonzalez: Thank you, John, for meeting with me. I know you are busy, so I will try to honor your time by being succinct. I have been looking over your failure rate and your common assessment scores, and I have a concern. As you can see by this graph I have created (Lever 4) from this year's data on your students, your failure rate for this past 6-week grading period is 36% for your students. Common assessments reflect that only 54% of your students are reaching the minimum performance standard in math at this time (Levers 1 and 2). The yearly state assessment is only 3 months away, and we need to make sure that more of your students show growth before then. I'm sure that this must be a concern for you as well (Lever 3).

John: Well, I supposed it is. I guess that I was actually happy that 54% of my students reached the minimum performance standard this time. As you can see by the graph, these results are actually up from 42% the last time that I gave the common assessments. And as far as my failure rate, I don't know what else to do. The students don't always bring their completed homework, and they sure don't want to stay after school for tutoring.

Ms. Gonzalez: What have you done as far as students who haven't brought homework or those students who need tutoring but haven't attended?

John: What do you mean?

Ms. Gonzalez: I mean, have you called home? Have you informed the parents that you are having these difficulties?

John: Well, not all of our parents speak English . . .

Ms. Gonzalez: If you will give me a list of names, I will be happy to call those with whom you are having difficulties (Lever 5). I will need to see a parent log of the calls that you made to the parents of students who do speak English the next time we meet. We need to keep our parents informed about both positive and negative classroom behaviors as much as possible. When can I expect the list of names for me to call?

John: Oh, okay, thank you! I'll try to have that for you by tomorrow morning. I'll also list the issue next to the student's name.

Ms. Gonzalez: That will be very helpful, thank you, John. Also, thanks for helping out with hall duty during the passing periods! You are one teacher I can count on every time to do that, without being reminded. That is why we have such few behavior issues at your end of the hallway (Lever 6). I can't thank you enough for that!

John: Hey, no problem! I actually get a lot out of being there, interacting with the students. I try to welcome my students as they come in into my classroom.

Ms. Gonzalez: That's an excellent practice, John! Before I let you go, tell me what you are doing as far as your failure rate. What plan will you be putting into place?

John: Well, I was planning on having a conference with each student that failed to not only talk about intervention plans but also show each one his or her longitudinal assessment data. Alice, my mentor teacher, told me that she does that and that it has really affected her students. She also gave me a copy of the contract that she and the students sign after their conference, which tells what intervention plan the student has agreed to do. I'm excited about having these conferences now!

Ms. Gonzalez: Alice is a new teacher to our building this year and seems to be bringing some excellent practices. Please let me know how these conferences go. If they have a positive impact on students, I may need you and Alice to present this to all our teachers. Now, don't let me keep you, since I know you have lots to do. I look forward to making those calls for you and hearing about those student conferences. Anytime that you are having issues with kids and I can help by calling parents, let me know.

John: Thanks, Ms. G!

Ms. Gonzalez: Goodbye, John!

Although this meeting was about a couple of negative performance issues, Ms. Gonzalez was able to keep the conversation positive and with resolution woven all the way through it. John left pumped up, ready to make a list of students for Ms. Gonzalez to call and ready to begin conferencing with his students who had failed. Ms. Gonzalez, John's assistant principal, monitors his accountability measures and addresses concerns that she has with him. John has a strong plan of action, which was validated in a positive way by his assistant principal. He left their conversation energized to implement it, instead of demoralized.

Now let's take this "changing minds" to a group level. During a faculty meeting, an administrator—the principal or an assistant principal—begins the discussion by showing campuswide data for ninth-grade students in failure rate, attendance, and grade point average by six weeks for the year. Mr. Lewis, the administrator presenting the common assessment data, flashes several slides showing the data. He then shares the research from a well-known Chicago study showing a direct correlation that ninth-grade students with low attendance, low grade point averages, and high failure rates also have high dropout rates (Levers 1 and 2).

He then refers them back to the slides of their own ninth-grade data and asks them to look at the slides through the lens of the Chicago study (Lever 4). After teachers discuss the data in small groups for a few minutes, Mr. Lewis asks for feedback (Levers 3 and 6). The teachers conclude that too many of their ninth graders are at-risk students or on a path to possibly become dropout students. Mr. Lewis asks what implications this has for the whole school. Teachers respond with the understanding that every grade level is affected when ninth graders do not succeed (Lever 6). Mr. Lewis then asks teachers to discuss possible interventions that the campus could implement to help at-risk ninth graders.

Intervention suggestions are shared, recorded, and prioritized. Implementation timelines are attached to the interventions that were decided on by the group (Lever 5). Campus administrators monitor the implementation of these interventions. After several weeks of implementation, administrators collect and share the resulting data to show the impact that interventions have on the at-risk students.

Negative situations can be turned into constructive, collaborative opportunities for growth. The way that the administrator handles the conversation is the key to whether the conversation goes well or escalates into a negative emotional outburst. Consider the following two scenarios: The first one shows the teacher's reaction to a difficult conversation escalating negatively; the second one shows the same issue but results in a positive outcome.

Mr. Washington: Hello, Ms. Luna, thanks for coming on time to our appointment.

Ms. Luna: I'm not sure what all this is about. Why do you want to see me?

Mr. Washington: Please, sit down. I'll be happy to explain. [*Mr. Washington gets out some documents.*] As you know, I have been popping into your classroom a lot during the last several weeks. I have noticed a few issues that I would like to address.

Ms. Luna: You are never in there very long . . .

Mr. Washington: Although I try to do longer observations in each of my classrooms at least once a week, the majority of time I go in for 3 to 7 minutes. As you know, teachers may see me coming in two to three times a week, so over time I pick up on patterns, some of which teachers may not be aware. For example, one of the concerns that I have about your classroom is that student engagement seems to be lacking. Often when I go in, I see you sitting at your desk, either grading papers or on the computer. Students are working on worksheets, and there just doesn't seem to be a lot of learning happening in there. It's also not unusual to see students with their heads down, even sleeping! Your low benchmark and common assessment data seem to support my conclusion.

Ms. Luna: It always seems like when you come in, you have just missed my lecture.

Mr. Washington: Ms. Luna, as I stated earlier, I am in there several times a week. I have trouble believing that I am always "just missing" your instruction.

Ms. Luna: Well, you are!

Mr. Washington: Ms. Luna, I have a growth plan that I want to put you on. It states that you must have increased student achievement in your classroom, not be seen sitting at your desk, and not letting students sleep in class. We will meet again in 3 weeks to go over my observations of your classroom that I will do between now and then, hopefully finding some positive change. Please sign your name right there indicating that you have received this plan.

Ms. Luna: Mr. Washington, I don't agree with this growth plan!

Mr. Washington: Ms. Luna, I understand that; however, it stands nonetheless. I will see you here again in 3 weeks. Have a good day. [*Teacher stalks off.*]

The conversation escalated from the onset. The assistant principal could have conveyed that the appointment was an opportunity for growth, as opposed to a personal attack. Here is the same scenario but with a positive outcome. Tone of voice is also different; one can hear it even though it is in written form. Listen carefully . . .

Mr. Washington: Hello, Ms. Luna, thanks for coming on time to our appointment.

Ms. Luna: I'm not sure what all this is about. Why do you want to see me?

Mr. Washington: Please, sit down. I'll be happy to explain. [*Mr. Washington gets out some documents.*] As you know, I have been popping into your classroom a lot during the last several weeks. As I have been going in there, I have noticed a few issues that I would like to address.

Ms. Luna: You are never in there very long . . .

Mr. Washington: Although I try to do longer observations in each of my class-rooms at least once a week, the majority of time I go in for 3 to 7 minutes. As you know, teachers may see me coming in two to three times a week, so over time I pick up on patterns, some of which teachers may not be aware. For example, one of the concerns that I have about your classroom is that student engagement seems to be lacking. Often when I go in, I see you sitting at your desk, either grading papers or on the computer. I'm not seeing a lot of group work, which has been one of our campus initiatives this year. I am also seeing students working on worksheets, which surprises me a bit since we just finished the book study on "Worksheets Don't Grow Dendrites." Can you help me understand what I'm seeing?

Ms. Luna: It always seems like when you come in, you have just missed my lecture . . . and the kids don't work well in groups. They talk too much!

Mr. Washington: Ms. Luna, I want you to be successful, so what can I do so that we can get you more comfortable with group work and more hands-on, rigorous student work?

Ms. Luna: I told you! I tried group work, and it doesn't work with these types of students. Every time I try to do something halfway fun, the kids get out of control. They don't deserve it.

Mr. Washington: I'll tell you what. Let's come up with a plan together. If we know that we have to move teachers toward being more successful with group work and engaging activities, how do you think we can do this?

Ms. Luna: Well, is any other teacher having success with these same kids?

Mr. Washington: Actually, yes. We have Mr. Knight and Ms. Parker who have your students in different periods. Would you want to observe them?

Ms. Luna: It wouldn't be a bad idea . . .

Mr. Washington: Good! What I need from you is a time that I can go in and take over your class for 30 minutes while you observe one of those teachers. Matter of fact, I'll be happy to cover your class the following week while you observe the second teacher as well. That way, you may observe a couple of different management styles. Also, you might want to pay attention to the instructional strategies that they are using. The only thing that I ask is that you share observation notes with me after each time you go. Is that fair?

Ms. Luna: I suppose . . .

Mr. Washington: Super! Now, please let me know by tomorrow what times would be good for me to cover your class. I really am looking forward to that part. Keeps my foot in the game, so to speak! Thanks for this opportunity.

Ms. Luna: Hey, no problem. Okay, I'll give you some times tomorrow. Thanks.

Mr. Washington: Look forward to it. See you tomorrow!

[*Teacher leaves, not quite sure what happened, but certainly more willing to participate in the plan than if it had been handled as in the previous scenario.*]

The administrator's job is not finished yet, though. Mr. Washington then goes to his computer and sends a letter to Ms. Luna via e-mail (see Textbox 8.1).

As noted, Mr. Washington has covered all the bases without causing the teacher to become defensive and therefore shut down. Instead, he uses collaboration. He asks her to help him come up with a plan together. He then states that she needs to create opportunities for group work and more hands-on, rigorous student work. He asks her how she might accomplish this. She really does not answer his question but deflects it by asking if other teachers are able to do group work with the same students. With his knowledge of his other teachers, Mr. Washington turned her question into a positive opportunity for her to observe other teachers who have had success with those students.

Now, why send the e-mail? This documenting practice is a win-win for everyone. First, if the teacher follows through on her plan, then the e-mail is

---

Textbox 8.1. Follow-Up E-Mail 1

Dear Ms. Luna,

As per our conversation today in my office, you have agreed to visit Ms. Knight and Mr. Parker (one this week and one next week) to look for how they are engaging students instructionally and for classroom management techniques. I volunteered to cover your class for both those 30-minute visits, so please get me a list of times that I can chose from to come by and cover for you while you observe other teachers this week and next. You also agreed to share your observation notes with me within 24 to 48 hours so that we can discuss what you observed.

Your willingness to observe other teachers speaks highly to your desire to add capacity to yourself. Our campus and our students need teachers who are willing to do that. Thank you, and I look forward to covering your class soon!

Mr. Washington

P.S. Take pity on me and remember, I am not an algebra teacher, so please find times that I can cover your classes without embarrassing myself too much in front of the students! ☺

---

perceived as a pat on the back. If the teacher does not follow though on what she said she was going to do, then it becomes part of the documentation to either help her grow . . . or go.

Administrators who regularly go into classrooms allow teachers the opportunity to go observe other teachers. When administrators regularly visit classrooms, it creates credibility with teachers and staff about that administrator's instructional intent. Through the consistent walk-throughs and formative assessments, it shows that the administrator is serious about helping the teacher develop stronger skills in a challenging area.

When done regularly, taking over classrooms allows the administrators to develop a different type of relationship with students. Students enjoy having the campus administrators come in and "take over." Most students always enjoy a change of face and pace. When parents hear from their students about administrators coming in and "teaching," it makes them sit up and notice. Over time, the culture of that campus becomes one with everybody on board to help students and teachers, which eventually is not only expected but bragged about by teachers and parents to stakeholders from other schools.

In this next scenario, the administrator comes up with a wonderful solution to covering the teacher's class. Also, the administrator asks Ms. Luna to share her observation notes from each teacher whom she visited while Mr. Washington was covering her class. He does this so that he can get a feel for what Ms. Luna saw and write those new techniques and strategies down on paper so that they can decide together which ones she will begin implementing in her classroom. The scenario looks something like this:

Mr. Washington: Thanks again for meeting with me, Ms. Luna. I sure enjoyed covering your class while you were observing! You have some real characters in that room! I have especially liked getting to know Jose, Pam, and Laquita better. I had been having some less-than-positive interactions with them outside of class, but while I was in there, we seemed to connect a bit better, so thanks for that opportunity. Please let me cover your class again in the future.

Ms. Luna: Um, sure. The students did mention that they enjoyed having you in there. They couldn't believe you could teach!

Mr. Washington: Thanks for giving me an algebra activity that I could actually do! Fake it till you make it, right? So tell me what you observed while you were in Ms. Parker's and Mr. Knight's rooms.

Ms. Luna: As I mentioned last week after the first visit, I saw Mr. Knight doing group work in his science class. He had a worksheet for his science problems, but I saw that he had trained the students to follow a certain procedure as they worked out the problem. He had "doctored" the worksheet such that the students had to draw a picture in one section, put the formula in another, and then explain how they got the answer in the last section. He gives two grades: one for the work and one for the answer. So if a student got the answer wrong, as long as he or she had attempted to find the answer by drawing the picture and all that, credit was still given. I am definitely bringing that back to my classroom. I can easily adapt that into my math class.

Mr. Washington: Okay, I can hear your enthusiasm for this strategy. What else did you see?

Ms. Luna: I saw the students in groups, asking for peer help if something wasn't understood. I heard students really talking about science, about what they didn't understand. And these are my same students. I don't get it.

Mr. Washington: What did you see in Ms. Parker's class?

Ms. Luna: Her social studies class was amazing! She had stations around the classroom. The students were sectioned off into five groups. Each student in the group had a job. There was a leader, a recorder, a time keeper, and so forth. Each group started at a different station. Each station had a different question about what it was studying, but the answer to the question had to be discussed in the group and then written down by the recorder. At the end of the five stations, each group shared its answer. The teacher kept a graphic organizer going on points where students agreed, disagreed, and so on. She was trying to show that not all problems have easy black-and-white solutions . . . because what has happened in the past, as far as wars and such, is not agreed on by everyone as to whether they were for the right reason. I couldn't believe these were the same students.

Mr. Washington: Why do you think the students were staying on task?

Ms. Luna: I have been really thinking about that. I have to admit it. I don't think I have challenged them mentally enough . . . or given them credit to be able to do these types of activities where they are moving around and talking to one another around a deep question. I talked with Marianne, my algebra partner, and she said that she has some stations activities for algebra. Who knew?

Mr. Washington: So are you going to try stations?

Ms. Luna: Yes, I think I will. I'm planning it out with Marianne tomorrow. I have to admit—I am cautiously excited. Um, do you think that you could watch her class for a few minutes the first period that I try this next week so that she can be in there with me?

Mr. Washington: As long as I have something to teach her students, it's a deal.

[*Ms. Luna leaves Mr. Washington's office enthused and hurries away to plan further.*]

Mr. Washington then sends out the follow-up e-mail (see Textbox 8.2).

Textbox 8.2. Follow-Up E-Mail 2

Ms. Luna,

Thank you for your receptiveness to the process of helping you gather additional skills in the areas of student engagement that leads to an increase in student management. Your enthusiasm speaks well of you.

As per our discussion today in my office, you have agreed to do a stations activity next week. I will cover Marianne's class first period for a few minutes while she helps you go through the stations activity with your students the first time you do it.

Thanks again for acting on the suggestions to make your class more engaging by embracing strategies that are more rigorous and hands-on. I look forward to professionally dialoguing with you about your experience!

Mr. Washington

The e-mail takes about 3 to 5 minutes to write, and it is important to write and send. Similar to why Mr. Washington sent the first one, this type of e-mail can send an encouraging thank-you or become part of the documentation that shows that the school did all it could to help a struggling teacher overcome his or her deficiencies, if the administration decides that it must release the teacher.

Learning how to say tough things to nice people with grace requires a change in thinking and in attitude. Instead of seeing it as something uncomfortable, approach it as the opportunity for growth that it actually is. An assistant principal must understand that by *not* having these conversations with the teacher, he or she is actually robbing the teacher of an opportunity to get better at his or her craft. It is a good idea to practice the conversation in one's own mind before having it with the employee.

Prepare for the different directions that the conversation could take. Done this way, it becomes a much more approachable exercise. Of course, the more that it is done, the easier it becomes. A savvy assistant principal role-plays typical scenarios with other administrators so that the activity becomes more comfortable and natural. Having this skill and using it help teachers "grow or go" can make an assistant principal an invaluable asset to a principal. It will also be a necessary asset when the principalship is finally attained.

A couple of scenarios are now listed. Practice orally with a partner or written out in script form. The conversation between you and the staff member is an important part of each scenario. Remember: The key is to stay professional and to work always toward de-escalating a situation so that it leads to a positive change.

Scenario 1. You are the administrator of an elementary school with 25 teachers. Most are female, but you do have 5 male teachers. Most of the teachers have worked together for several years. You recently find out that one of your best teachers, Ms. Wilson, wants to transfer from your campus because she is uncomfortable with the male teacher on her team, Mr. Warner.

a. Discuss with Ms. Wilson the reasons for her wanting a transfer to a nearby school.
b. What can you say to Ms. Wilson that might have her reconsidering her transfer?
c. What will you say to Mr. Warner, if anything?

Scenario 2. Ms. Ford, a second-year teacher, is creating wonderful lesson plans, which include everything that your lesson plan checklist requires. They are ready and open at her desk every Monday, as required by the Campus Teacher Handbook. However, you notice that she is rarely doing what her lesson plans say to do most of the times that you have come in to observe or check lesson plans. Even after the discussion about the need for differentiated instruction, she wrote it in her plans but did not do it in her classroom.

a. What are your first steps with Ms. Ford?
b. What kind of documentation do you need to do?
c. What do you say to Ms. Ford the second time that you notice that she has not followed through instructionally on what is in her lesson plans?

~

CHAPTER 9

Step 9:
Find a Principal Mentor

Assistant principals need to find a principal mentor who embodies the instructional leadership qualities that they want to emulate. Often, assistant principals, either officially or unofficially, have the building principal become their mentor, role modeling how to handle the everyday scenarios that affect campuses.

However, just as often, assistant principals find someone outside the school to be their principal mentor. Not only is this a wise practice, especially when an assistant principal's own building principal is not strong instructionally, but it provides another role model and networking opportunities. When it is time for assistant principals to put their names in the hat for the principalship, it is a huge benefit if their mentor is well known in the school district.

The business world has long understood the need for mentor relationships. Myriad books and websites are devoted to the value of mentoring and how to sustain mentoring relationships. Per Allen in About.com, a website for entrepreneurs, a mentor is someone with more administrative experience who serves as a trusted confidante over an extended period:

> Why do [mentors] do this? First and foremost, as a way of giving back to their community and to society at large. They may do it to develop their skills as a teacher, manager, strategist, or consultant. And a true mentoring relationship also works in both directions—they learn about new ideas from you just as you learn timeless wisdom from them. (Allen, n.d.-a)

It is important to acknowledge that the principal mentor receives as much from a good mentor–mentee relationship as the mentee. The benefits for an assistant principal include the following:

- Be able to learn from others' mistakes and successes by tapping into an experienced administrator. Their role is to share lessons from their experience in the hopes that others can avoid the pitfalls that often await new administrators. This type of professional advice is virtually priceless coming from a longtime effective principal. To judge this, look at the school's performance data over the last few years, the campus's state and federal accountability status, and the teacher turnover rate, if possible. Those alone are good indicators of a strong, effective principal.
- Have access to a more extensive network. The principal mentor, being an experienced administrator, is likely to have a larger district network and can offer access to other opportunities that might otherwise be unknown.
- Have a trusted long-term relationship. As the relationship develops over time, trust can grow even stronger. As the principal mentor gets to know his or her mentee, he or she can become a valuable sounding board for new ideas before taking them to the campus principal. This allows the ideas to become better developed simply by discussing them. Over time, the principal mentor becomes more effective in giving feedback as he or she becomes more familiar with the mentee's skill sets.

There are many rewards to being in a strong mentor relationship, especially when it benefits both parties. How can the right principal mentor be found? It all depends on how well connected an assistant principal is. For example, an assistant principal in a large district may have very little problem finding a suitable principal mentor due to the large number of administrators in that district. In a smaller district, however, an assistant principal may have to go outside the district in search of a principal mentor. Figure 9.1 lists some steps one can take in finding the right principal mentor.

Once you have found candidates for prospective mentors, here are some recommendations that will help whittle your list down to the perfect one:

List three goals for the principal mentor–mentee relationship.

List prospective principal mentors, and research available information about them.

Get ideas from other trusted professional acquaintances for more candidates.

In the Assistant Principal's School District

> Often an assistant principal can find a suitable principal mentor within his or her own organization, or through the AP's own building principal.

In a Neighboring School District

> Many times an assistant principal needs to reach out to a principal in another school district.

Through Professional Educational Organizations

> Some professional associations offer principal mentoring programs. Many larger districts have administrator organizations that meet monthly after work. See if there is such an opportunity or suggest to your professional educational organization that a mentoring program be started!

From Direct Personal Contact

> Assistant principals should explore their networks of former bosses, people they met through professional associations, networking groups, or online educational social networks.

➤ The principal mentor should be someone admired and respected, and preferably who has already been a role model.

➤ He or she could be a principal who has already been helpful on a smaller scale who might be willing to formalize a more in-depth relationship.

➤ Don't forget that a principal mentor can come from the ranks of central office administrators that were once admired principals. Don't limit the search to only "active principals".

Figure 9.1.   Steps to finding the right principal mentor.

E-mail the principal mentor prospects most aligned with your goals to request a meeting.

Call to set an appointment.

Prepare a short list of questions regarding your current situation, future career goals, and timelines on which to get their feedback.

Meet with them at the set time.

State your mission to find a principal mentor.

Share your goals and questions.

Be sure to take notes on any suggestions and advice!

Ask about the possibility of entering into a long-term mentee–mentor relationship, if the conversation went well.

Send a thank-you note.

Take action on their suggestions.

Call to set up another appointment, and be ready to discuss the results of the suggested actions.

During a second meeting, suggest a set time to meet (e.g., every 3–4 weeks, with an action plan attached to each meeting to help lead the discussion).

A principal mentor can become not only an advisor but a friend and confidante. It does not happen instantly, as building trust and personal interest takes time. Setting the tone at the outset of the relationship by demonstrating commitment to the process is the building block to a successful mentor–mentee relationship.

Noah Cirincione of Advance Mentoring, a service that helps locate business mentors, discusses establishing a foundation to build a solid principal mentoring relationship. Cirincione says that consistency and groundwork are critical: "Frequency of contact is important in the relationship to keep the learning process moving forward. Each new discussion with the mentor should include updates from the mentee on items the mentor recommended in the previous talk" (Allen, n.d.-b).

The principal mentor must be involved in the big picture, not just the details. Working to set the mentee's goals should be kept as the crucial reason for meeting. Not only should the principal mentor–mentee talk about current issues, but they should also focus on making sure that the short- and long-term goals are being carried out. Remember to come to every meeting prepared. Bring pen and paper, PDA, laptop, and even a voice recorder. Review notes from previous meetings, and update action items based on their status. Bring the notes to the next meeting for discussion.

There is more to an effective principal mentoring relationship than organized meetings, though. Denise Michaels, a marketing expert and best-selling business author who has mentored hundreds of entrepreneurs, has recommendations on how to succeed on the interpersonal aspects of the mentoring relationship:

- Take an interest in the mentor as a human being. Do not let the relationship be all one-sided. Ask questions about his or her current goals. Follow up every once in a while on the status of those goals.
- Do not say, "I'd like to pick your brain." Instead, say, "I would really value your opinion."

- Do not try to monopolize a lot of your mentor's time. Connect in a way that's quick and easy. If a morning meeting is planned, ask what he or she likes in his or her coffee or tea, bring a Starbucks and get 15 quality minutes.
- Be clear about what you're doing and what you need. Work on developing a clear elevator speech and mission statement. Think about one or two specific questions that need answering and think about how to ask those questions clearly.
- Listen, listen, listen to what they say. Do not think about all the reasons why it can't work. Instead, say, "I'm dealing with yada, yada, yada—how would you suggest overcoming those obstacles?"
- Thank the person for their time. Tell them what is going on and then when action is taken. Be sure to let them know what is happening.
- Reciprocate once in awhile. Send a great article that the mentor would enjoy with a quick note. Offer to help him or her out in some way. Do not say, "How can I help you?" Then they have to figure it out. Say, "I'm really very good at _____. If you ever need _____, give me a call, I'll be more than happy to help out any way I can." Even if he never takes you up on it, he will appreciate your offer.

Learn to make the link between cause and effect. The job of a mentor is not to take assistant principals by the hand every step of the way. It is to give them some guidance as they are on their way. The assistant principals' job is to make the link between what they are told and how they will apply it to their life.

With mutual respect, demonstrated through action as well as attitude, the principal mentoring relationship can be mutually rewarding. For aspiring principals, it is important to learn from the best. The learning should include not only talking with the mentor but actually implementing the recommendations from him or her. That way, an ambitious assistant principal arrives into the principalship more fully prepared for the position.

CHAPTER 10

~

Step 10:
Avoid Burnout:
Lead a Balanced Life

The only people without stress are in the cemetery!

—Swick (1987)

The single most powerful investment we can ever make in life is the investment in ourselves—the only instrument we have with which to deal with life and to contribute.

—Stephen Covey

Life on today's campuses, especially at the secondary level, can be pressure filled and hectic. The accountability era has left administrators, teachers, and students frazzled and test tired. It is not enough anymore for a campus to be successful academically; it must also know where each student is, even if one drops out at the "adult" age of 18 years to pursue a job. Parents demand immediate attention. Students respond in negative ways to policies and rules that were once everyday no-no's, such as cell phone use, dress code, piercings, and tattoos. The pace is often frantic more than just hurried. The expectations from the principal are that assistant principals are everywhere and do everything. The parents want their children treated as if they are more special than other kids, and kids just want everyone to just leave them alone. Whew! How does one cope?

Figure 10.1 has a "coping" questionnaire. Circle yes or no to each of the 10 questions.

Take a minute to answer a few of the following questions:		
1. Do you tire more easily and/or feel fatigued rather than energetic?	Y	N
2. Are people telling you "you look tired"?	Y	N
3. Are you working harder but getting less and less done?	Y	N
4. Are you increasingly pessimistic and disillusioned?	Y	N
5. Are you forgetting appointments, missing deadlines, or losing things?	Y	N
6. Are people accusing you of being irritable? More short-tempered?	Y	N
7. Are you becoming more and more disappointed in the people around you?	Y	N
8. Are you too busy to do everyday things like make phone calls, read reports, or read/send emails?	Y	N
9. Are you suffering from physical issues, such as aches, pains, headaches, or lingering cold symptoms?	Y	N
10. Have you stopped being able to laugh at yourself?	Y	N

Figure 10.1. Coping questionnaire. *Source*. Adapted from *The Secrets of Executive Success* (Golin, Briklin, & Diamond, 1991).

If you answered yes to more than two or three of the coping questions, it may be time to slow down and reflect. Many coping strategies are outlined in this book. Organizing oneself and becoming more internally disciplined are effective coping methods to deal with the frantic pace in schools today. Working with a goal in mind and working with a mentor are ways to keep from losing sight of the principalship dream.

However, *saying* and *doing* are two different things. Many people start New Year's resolutions with the best intention to eat right and exercise regularly, but few people follow through and make their resolutions part of a lifelong plan for good health. The same is true for the steps found in this book. Reading these chapters, following the suggestions, and taking action are essential if an assistant principal is to reach the principalship in tip-top, effective instructional and operational shape. To become a stronger instructional leader requires practice, just like most things in life. Stress, if an administrator is not careful, can derail goals and ambitions more easily than thought.

The definition of stress has changed over the last hundred years, and the variations are endless, especially if many people are asked to give their definition. Psychologists, managers, and laypeople cannot agree on a single definition, because different people are affected by different experiences in different ways. The most common or accepted definition of stress, attributed to Richard S. Lazarus by several different sources, is "a condition or feeling experienced when a person perceives that the demands exceed the personal and social resources the individual is able to mobilize."

In other words, the stress level of a person is a direct correlation between what the situation is and what skills the person has to cope with it. Some people say that a little bit of stress is good because it keeps a mind sharp and focused. Nevertheless, the need for the skill sets discussed in this book become glaringly important as the effects of coping with stress and burnout are understood. As Maslach, Schaufeli, and Leiter (2001) in *Annual Review of Psychology* state, job burnout is

> a conceptualization of job burnout as a psychological syndrome in response to chronic interpersonal stressors on the job. The three key dimensions of this response are overwhelming exhaustion, feelings of cynicism and detachment from the job, and a sense of ineffectiveness and lack of accomplishment. The exhaustion component represents the basic individual stress dimension of burnout. It refers to feelings of being overextended and depleted of one's emotional and physical resources. The cynicism (or depersonalization) component represents the interpersonal context dimension of burnout. It refers to a negative, callous, or excessively detached response to various aspects of the job. The component of reduced effectiveness or accomplishment represents the self-evaluation dimension of burnout. It refers to feelings of incompetence and a lack of achievement and productivity at work.

In other words, busy administrators must be on the lookout in themselves (and others!) for the three key dimensions that may indicate that they are headed toward job burnout. Getting run down from days that are filled with frantic happenings on the campus and late nights supervising sports games and other campus events can lead to overwhelming exhaustion. Dealing with angry parents, apathetic students, and stubborn teachers can make administrators feel cynical and detached from their job. Certainly, a sense of ineffectiveness and a lack of accomplishment can come from not seeing immediate success with teachers and students despite an administrator's best efforts.

So how does one keep from burning out? The previous chapters provide nine steps to keep an assistant principal's passion burning instead of burning out. However, these steps are effective only if they are practiced faithfully. The important step in this chapter talks about keeping a balance between work and home life. Busy assistant principals must take time to take care of themselves.

Future principals easily neglect certain basic functions while on a campus, such as eating regularly, drinking sufficient water, getting enough exercise, and even going to the bathroom! Allowing basic functions to take a backseat to the crisis of the moment, especially when done on a frequent basis, can lead to an unhealthy body, mind, and future. When overwhelmed with late nights, Saturday school, paperwork, discipline issues, and textbook duties, the pull from home and family can add even more pressure and stress. The need to learn to balance family and work becomes even more significant.

"Burnout is easier to avoid than to cure," says Vanderbilt University researcher Wil Clouse (1999), creator of the Burnout Assessment Inventory. He suggests that administrators not take on too much too early. Assistant principals need to make these steps lifelong habits by choosing a few to focus on and then adding others as they become proficient in their implementation. Executing a few of the steps consistently is more effective than attempting to implement all of them sporadically. Learning how to maintain balance when embracing instructional leadership, managing other school duties, and being present for home life is a valuable practice.

Allan Forbis (2003), author of *Avoiding the Slow Burn . . . Are You a Candidate for Professional Burnout?* talks about self-preservation factors that can be used to protect against the "burn." These factors are presented in Figure 10.2.

As pointed out by Forbis, the best defense against job burnout is one's own mental capacity to understand how to keep from getting burned out. On careful perusal of the self-preservation factors that can be used to protect against the burn, all involve personal reflection, and a few involve choosing to view difficult situations positively.

The synthesis of the research suggests that to avoid getting disillusioned or burned out by their job, busy administrators must take care of themselves. They can do this by

- Taking care of basic functions, such as eating regularly, drinking sufficient water, getting enough exercise, and even going to the bathroom while on campus
- Going to the doctor for regular check-ups each year
- Taking a 15-minute break at least once a day
- Leaving work issues at work as much as possible so that they do not interfere with home life
- Staying internally disciplined by following the steps in this book
- Having a hobby that occupies attention when not at work
- Working on staying positive even when the environment is negative

This last point is important: Studies show that a positive attitude has a healthy effect on a person. Positive attitudes also influence other people and tone down the negative feelings or vibes that occur in difficult situations. Being positive is contagious! An administrator with a positive attitude in an

SELF-PRESERVATION FACTORS
SPF1
Be your biggest fan. One of the biggest causes of burnout is a lack of feedback from people whose opinion matter. Give yourself a positive "pep talk" when the job is done if no one else will.
SPF2
Control what's best in you. Burnout happens when someone gets fixated on only the results and not on the effort. You may feel helpless in the face of having7 done an outstanding job, but for whatever reason, something just didn't work out. See SPF1!
SPF3
You are what you think. Burnout can emanate from your own ideas about what you think is going on rather than from what is actually happening. Approach the tasks you must do at work as having value or challenging, rather than as a pain in the neck.
SPF4
You can't always be perfect. The biggest pressures many face in their job are those that they bring on themselves. Perfectionism can be a huge roadblock to maintaining a healthy perspective on your work.
SPF5
Give yourself a break. Many supervisors and managers believe that only "employees" take breaks. Remember, the more hours you work, the less effective and efficient you become. To maintain peak performance–sanity–take a 15 minute break during the day.
SPF6
Focus on priorities. Confusion, frustration and burnout can happen to anyone who does not have a clear picture of what they need and want to do in life. Set aside some time to write a personal goal statement for both home and work.
SPF7
Learn and improve. If you feel an inability to get ahead, or at least surviving at work is causing you a great deal of anxiety or frustration, pinpoint the skills you need and then figure out how to get them.
SPF8
Start your own business on company time. Just think of your job and your team as a company–your company–with you as its sole owner. Ask yourself, what can you do to improve your team's success ratio? What strengths can you help other team members develop? Exploring the answers to these questions is a great way to bring new energy into your job and your team.
SPF9
Move on. This is often the first reaction. However, in practical terms, it should always be the last. Don't immediately toss aside your job just because you think the "grass is greener" somewhere else. It seldom is.

Figure 10.2. Self-preservation factors to protect against the "burn." *Source. Avoiding the Slow Burn* (Forbis, 2003).

environment such as a low-performing school can be a ray of sunshine for hardworking staff.

An assistant principal who is on track for the principalship must learn how to balance work and home so that he or she stays healthy, positive, and eager to learn. As mentioned previously, waiting until one has assumed the principalship is not the time to begin learning how to avoid burnout. Learning to balance life is a skill that must be developed before becoming a principal and then continued to be worked on as a lifelong habit. Taking care of oneself is the first step to being able to handle administrative duties successfully.

CHAPTER 11

~

Sum It Up

Assistant principals have now read about the 10 steps to becoming a stronger instructional leader in anticipation of assuming the principalship. Although it may seem like many steps to learn, they are all in fact related in some way to one another. Chapter 1, "Understand School Accountability Systems," is not just about the state and federal accountability policies. Accountability systems relate to assessments, which have to do with the curriculum and how it is taught. Chapter 3, "Increase Instructional Leadership Capacity," helps an aspiring principal understand how the structures of the written, taught, and tested curriculum all work together.

Monitoring all systems is an essential piece for administrators, but disciplining oneself to do this on a busy campus takes reflection and effort, which are embedded throughout the book. The chapters on setting goals and being organized have a direct impact on classroom instruction, especially when combined with effective communication, as mentioned in chapter 8, "Say Tough Things to Nice People With Grace."

Points and concepts from one chapter directly influence the points and concepts in another, so viewing the chapters in isolation cannot and should not be done. Having said that, I think it can be daunting to embrace all 10 steps at the same time. Chunking up the work, so to speak, is an excellent way to start. Moreover, many aspiring principals reading this book have some of these steps already under their belts.

Suggestions on how to begin the work of following the steps in this book include the following:

- Find a group of assistant principals to join a book study. Book study groups promote conversations among people who lead the application of new ideas and improvement of existing skills. The study group can focus on issues related to school change and help build community among its participants. Some districts will allow employees to use book study groups to earn professional development credit or hours.
- Work with a mentor to go through the book together. Work on projects (e.g., becoming more educationally literate), attend PLCs, set walk-through goals, and then discuss the outcomes.
- Work with the building principal—if different from the mentor—to go through the book together. As in the second suggestion, work on projects, attend PLCs, set walk-through goals, and then discuss the outcomes.
- Create a group of teachers who want or are currently working on their administrative certificate, and start a book study.
- Go to the Askdrbgood.com blog and join the online discussion on the different chapters in the book.
- Create your own blog, and discuss the book online with other aspiring administrators and future principals.

Book study activities might include the following:

- Present a chapter each week. Depending on the size of the book study, chapters could be team taught.
- Begin the following week by reviewing the previous chapter with a "quick write" reflection activity. Participants write how they implemented the ideas from the previous week and the results that occurred.
- Present with a hands-on activity embedded within the presentation that includes all participants. Presentations should not be all lecture.
- Embed relevant video clips into the presentations where possible to help enhance participants' instructional technology skills and make the presentation more engaging.
- Center the presentation on one or two questions vital to the main points of the chapter.
- Begin the presentation with a K-W-L chart (know, want to know, learned) or other graphic organizers. End the presentation with the "What have you learned?" column of the K-W-L chart.

- Leave participants with the answer to "What will this look like on my campus?" or "What will this look like for me?" at the end of the presentation.

After the book study is concluded, follow up with the main learning points. Elect a leader who will do this follow-up. The group should evaluate the book. Participants should ask themselves, "What will we continue to do with the information that we have learned from this book?" Think about what types of follow-ups are needed to implement changes and support study group members. Have each participant create an action plan, outlining which steps need more attention for himself or herself.

Plan to gather again at a certain point—4 weeks after finishing the book study, for example—to examine the impact of these changes outlined in the action plans. The group should choose to continue meeting after having read the book to discuss how it has changed its instructional leadership practices. The group should also decide to continue to meet and read more books on a similar or another needed topic.

An aspiring principal should not go through the entire book alone. Feedback, as mentioned in several chapters, is an effective growth tool. Collaborative and reflective opportunities with others help process concepts at a deeper level. Educational research emphasizes the need for collaborative environments, and this work requires it as well.

With today's available technology, options are available even if an assistant principal cannot find a person or group of persons with whom to conduct a book study. Educational websites abound, and taking part in one or more of them should become a norm for all administrators. As talked about in chapter 7, "Embrace Instructional Technology," a principal must role-model the use and expectation of instructional technology to his or her staff. This means embracing it as an assistant principal so that by the time one becomes principal, it is a normal and natural skill set.

The title of this book, *Beyond Books, Butts, and Buses: Ten Steps to Help Assistant Principals Become Effective Instructional Leaders*, emphasizes the instruction side of an administrator's job. That is not to say that there are no operational duties as well. As discussed in several chapters, good administrators are able to blend both sides so that each is done well. Effective principals are both strong instructional leaders and good managers. However, these skills must be developed *before* assuming the role of principal, instead of waiting to develop them after becoming principal.

Almost all these chapters require learning or strengthening skills as an ongoing task. That is, an assistant principal cannot just understand today's accountability system and check that off the list. Once it is learned, it must be followed up by reading educational news items on what the federal and state governments are changing to further affect educational reform. As noted in chapter 1, "Understand School Accountability Systems," even as this book was being written, changes to NCLB were being considered. By the time that this book is printed and in the hands of readers, laws may have been passed that drastically change the current federal educational environment.

Chapter 2, "Stay Current With Educational Trends," also emphasizes the need to know what researchers are currently saying about instructional practices in successful schools. Reading (or, as we now are able to do, listening!) to educational journals should become a norm in an administrator's life. Whether it is taking an hour at home each weekend or listening in the car to something downloaded to the MP3 player or cell phone, it is a must for all effective administrators.

The chapters on understanding the written, taught, and tested curriculum by either bringing in PLCs or making sure that the current ones are running more effectively cannot be ignored. It is only through this structure, when executed faithfully, that learning at the teacher and administrator levels happens. When administrators and teachers collaboratively look at data in the form of student work products, assessment data, and so forth, this leads to professional dialogue, reflection, and, ultimately, an understanding that an instructional concept may need to be taught differently.

If the data show that the impact of the instruction on students did not garner the results wanted, then two things have been learned. One, what do the teachers have to do differently to reach those who did not learn the concept? Second, what groups of students need interventions so that they can gain the needed concept and catch up with those who got it the first time? It is high time that PLCs move from just being thought of as a compliance item ("I gotta go to PLCs, sigh . . .") to a valued practice ("Can we meet again after school so that we can keep discussing what interventions we are going to put in for this last group of hard-to-move students?").

Learning to communicate more proficiently—chapter 8, "Say Tough Things to Nice People With Grace"—is a skill that takes time to develop. New situations pop up each week that administrators could not have anticipated, so practicing using the scenarios listed in the chapter can go a long way toward helping build the capacity to confront the tough issues with professionalism. Role-playing different scenarios with a mentor, a book study group, or another aspiring principal should be an ongoing exercise to strengthen this skill.

Finally, making sure that busy administrators take time to care for themselves is imperative, as mentioned in chapter 10, "Avoid Burnout." Eating, sleeping, exercising, and drinking enough water sound like givens, but many an administrator have fallen prey to sickness and weariness for not taking care of those basic needs. Learning to balance home and school is a careful dance that must be learned before becoming principal.

Final Thoughts

The key thread that has been woven throughout every chapter is the need to monitor the daily and weekly commitments that an ambitious assistant principal has vowed to do. Monitor the PLCs. Follow through on the classroom goals set for each week. If a project was started to help develop a skill mentioned in this book—for example, Model 1 or Model 2 from chapter 3—see it all the way through. Attend the professional development that will strengthen the content area being supervised. Are teacher growth plans being worked so that teachers receive feedback and monitoring in a timely fashion? Not getting derailed is part of being organized and developing internal discipline.

The second key thread is to monitor what others should be doing under that administrator's watch. Follow through on making sure that the PLC agenda for the content area being supervised reflects only instructional items and activities, not departmental ones. Is the PLC binder being kept up-to-date with signature pages, agendas, and minutes of each meeting? Are teachers implementing the instructional strategies discussed in the PLCs? Are teachers being monitored for having current work on walls, easily available portfolios, and up-to-date student profiles? Are teachers using rigorous, engaging instructional activities? Are the common assessments showing students are learning?

Monitoring is the key piece to all the activity that goes on in campuses and classrooms, yet it is the least observed or followed through. It is my contention that if every campus administrator, from principal on down, monitored the operational and instructional systems in the school, teacher capacity would go through the roof, as would student test scores.

The evidence for this can be shown by the many schools nationwide that have figured this out. Yes, it would be nice to have more parent and community involvement. It is important and certainly beneficial to any campus lucky enough to have it. But we cannot let ourselves be held hostage to what we do not currently have. Look at what is there, then work to improve it by collaborating with the best minds around: those of the teachers!

Being a principal can be the best of worlds or the worst of worlds . . . much depends on the level of preparation before reaching the position. Ambitious assistant principals find that taking on these 10 steps a year or two before assuming the principalship will make their first year a much more seamless transition into being *the* instructional leader of the campus.

Today's campuses need leaders who are educated in the practices that lead to increased teacher and student growth and achievement. Understanding the need to be a lifelong learner and then becoming one will help aspiring assistant principals develop into the strong instructional leaders that our campuses must have to be successful in this intense age of accountability.

APPENDIX A

~

Vocabulary Strategies

Vocabulary Card Game

On the front of 32 index cards, write different vocabulary words having to do with this unit or semester's concept. On the back of each word, write the definition. Shuffle the stack like a deck of cards.

1. Deal 4 cards per player.
2. Put the rest of the cards face down on the table.
3. Each player matches a word with its correct definition in his or her hand and then puts the pair of words down on a table.
4. On each turn, the player must match a word with its definition, or else the player can pick a card from the other person's deck or pick from the top of the deck.
5. If someone gets a pair, he or she gets another turn. If not, the next player takes a turn.
6. Keep playing until all the cards are used up from the deck on the table and there are no more pairs to be made.

The game is won by the most number of pairs made. Each pair is worth 2 points. If it results in a match, he or she can put the pair down for 2 points. Guaranteed to make students beg to play again, especially if a sweet treat is offered as a prize.

Clues and Answers

1. Distribute several index cards to each student.
2. Have students print vocabulary words on their index cards selected from the current unit of study. Each student will have words that are different from those of other students.
3. Have the students write on a separate sheet of paper questions (clues) that their words could answer. This teaches the students to write higher-level thinking questions.
4. Check the students' questions for accuracy.
5. The students print the approved questions on the other side of their index cards.
6. Student use the completed index cards to quiz one another. They read the clues (questions) and have other students determine the words on the cards.

Example
Word: amendment (to the U.S. Constitution).
Questions (clues):

- "What are changes in, or additions to, a constitution called?"
- "What must be proposed by a two-thirds vote of both houses of Congress or at the request of two-thirds of the state legislatures?"
- "What must be ratified by approval of three-fourths of the states?"

This activity is a good one to use during the last 5 to 7 minutes of class before the bell rings.

"Other Half" Activity

Have students neatly write the selected vocabulary terms on index cards and the definitions on other index cards.

1. Pass out a card with a term to one half the class and the definition to the other half.
2. At the teacher's command, have the students search and find their "other half."
3. When students have found their other half, they should show it by using a preapproved sign, such as one student placing his or her fist on top of the other half's fist.

4. Activity stops when all the students have found their other half.
5. The pairs should then give their word and definition, with the class verifying the match.

The cards can be redistributed and the game replayed, or it can be played as a bell ringer at the start of class.

Vocabulary/Concepts Images Activity

1. Select three or four visuals that include most of the critical vocabulary words for the current or upcoming unit.
2. Provide hard-copy selected images to students from the current unit's concepts/vocabulary.
3. Project the visuals on a screen one at a time, and identify the words that describe or define the image.
4. Have students label the image on their hard copies with the appropriate vocabulary words and definitions.
5. The next day, project the images on a screen and ask students to identify key concepts/vocabulary by displaying the images one at a time.

The second-day activity can be used as a bell-ringer or warm-up activity. This can be done also as a review a couple of days before the test.

Role-Playing Activity

If historical figures are included as vocabulary, have students role-play by acting out and providing dialogue in 30 seconds. Students can pair up and research a historical figure, writing a script that they will then use to act out in front of the class. Students should also try to use other vocabulary words (e.g., a minimum of five words) from the current unit of study to integrate it into their script. The teacher should grade the presentation based on accuracy and use of the vocabulary words.

"Don't Know/Now Know" Activity

This activity is an excellent preassessment of student content knowledge before the study of a new unit. From the upcoming unit, choose several vocabulary words that have proven to be hard to remember by students in the past. It can also be used as a review for an upcoming assessment to check for understanding.

Have students make a chart with the column headings shown in Table A1.1.

Table A1.1. Chart for "Don't Know/Now Know" Activity

Word	A	B	C	D	Meaning
	I know the meaning, and I use the word.	I know the meaning, but I don't use the word.	I've seen the word before, but I don't really know it.	I've never seen the word before.	
Example: ratify			√		

1. Students will copy each word in the first column of the chart and check the appropriate category (A, B, C, or D) for each word.
2. Students will write the meanings of as many vocabulary words as they know in the *Meaning* column.
3. After they have filled in the chart, break them into groups and ask them to share with one another the meanings they are confident about.
4. They can copy meanings from other students during this time for those words they do not know.
5. Review the charts with them, answer any questions, and give them additional information or help clarify words with which they still have difficulty.

Synonym Activity

Each day, students encounter new words that they may not understand. When one teaches meanings for critical words, it is important to connect them to their readings.

1. Select two or three vocabulary words in text that students will have difficulty understanding.
2. Find three text passages where the meaning of the words can be clearly understood.
3. Provide students the three passages.
4. Ask them to replace the word being studied with a synonym that carries the same meaning. They can use a thesaurus, the computer, or other students to seek synonyms.

Through the study of multiple reading passages and synonyms, students will become more comfortable with the vocabulary terms and less likely to stumble over them when reading other social studies passages.

Example

For the word *ratify*, find three passages that use the term in the same context.

Students who study the passages and the different definitions of the word will find that substituting the synonyms "approve," "sanction," and "endorse" will help them become more fluent readers and comprehend text better.

Frayer Model

1. Assign a concept or word being studied.
2. Model how to fill out the diagram (see Figures A1.1 and A1.2).
3. Provide students with time to practice with assigned terms.
4. Once the diagram is complete, let students share their work with one another. Have students keep their different models in a binder as a "dictionary" that they can refer back on when studying for the upcoming test or other activities.

Definition (in own words)	Characteristics
Word	
Examples (from own life)	Nonexamples (from own life)

Figure A1.1.

Definition	Characteristics
(in own words)	
The ideas, beliefs, and ways of doing things that a group of people who live in an area share	Shared ideas, Shared beliefs, Shared practices

Culture

Examples	Nonexamples
(from own life)	(from own life)
"What my friends and I wear" "Music we listen to"	Color of my hair Color of my eyes Nature The weather

Figure A1.2.

APPENDIX B

~

Bloom's Taxonomy

In 1956, Benjamin Bloom headed a group of educational psychologists who developed a classification of levels of intellectual behavior important in learning. During the 1990s, a new group of cognitive psychologists, led by Lorin Anderson (a former student of Bloom), updated the taxonomy reflecting relevance to 21st-century work. Figure B1.1 represents the new verbiage associated with the long-familiar Bloom's taxonomy. Note the change from nouns to verbs to describe the different levels of the taxonomy. Note also that the top two levels are essentially exchanged from the old version to the new.

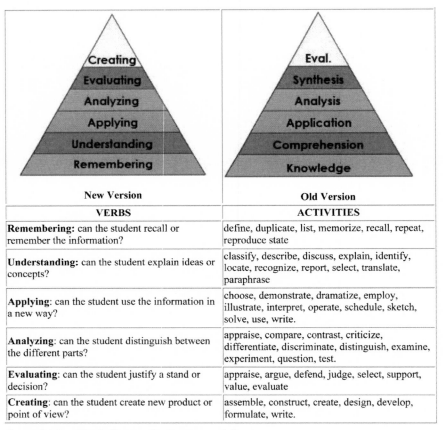

New Version	Old Version
VERBS	ACTIVITIES
Remembering: can the student recall or remember the information?	define, duplicate, list, memorize, recall, repeat, reproduce state
Understanding: can the student explain ideas or concepts?	classify, describe, discuss, explain, identify, locate, recognize, report, select, translate, paraphrase
Applying: can the student use the information in a new way?	choose, demonstrate, dramatize, employ, illustrate, interpret, operate, schedule, sketch, solve, use, write.
Analyzing: can the student distinguish between the different parts?	appraise, compare, contrast, criticize, differentiate, discriminate, distinguish, examine, experiment, question, test.
Evaluating: can the student justify a stand or decision?	appraise, argue, defend, judge, select, support, value, evaluate
Creating: can the student create new product or point of view?	assemble, construct, create, design, develop, formulate, write.

Figure B1.1. Blank diagram for Frayer model.

APPENDIX C

~

Student Accommodations Plan for English-Language Learners

Student Accommodations Plan for English-Language Learners

_____, an English-language learner, will receive the following classroom accommodations for the _____ school year:

Writing/Vocabulary Accommodations

____ Reduced note taking
____ Student vocabulary translations, illustrations for resource/pictures/video
____ Completion activities with graphs, charts, and maps
____ Vocabulary matching/fill-in-the-blank exercises with word list
____ Questions with short answers/clues given (written exercises)
____ Working with partner/cooperative learning group when paragraph, synthesizing, or summarizing
____ Definitions of vocabulary before a topic is discussed
____ Use of study skills class to improve content retention/understanding
____ Oral/written inventory of key vocabulary using the following:
    ____ Cassette tapes
    ____ Flash cards
    ____ Dictionary/Pictionary
    ____ Manipulatives
    ____ Focus on sight word vocabulary (elementary)
    ____ Journal writing

___ Manuscript fonts
___ Less information on a page
___ Various learning styles

Instruction and Test-Taking Accommodations

___ Reduce number of questions to be answered/marked
___ Prioritize instructional standards/objectives
___ Reduce choices on multiple-choice tests
___ Indicate page numbers to answer next to the question
___ A lot more time for reading assignments and/or shorten amount of material to be covered
___ Rephrase questions and directions
___ Use fill-in-the-blank tests/worksheets with vocabulary list provided
___ Utilize group projects rather than individual work
___ Give open-book tests
___ Reduce the number of matching options
___ Answer questions on test; avoid use of machine-scored answer sheets
___ Give test over several days or in sections
___ Present test questions in same phrasing as used in learning/review

Reading Accommodations

Nonreaders will

___ Use pictures
___ Use stories, read aloud, and use gestures, objects, or drama
___ Use poetry: recite or memorize
___ Provide real experience
___ Play word games
___ Create chart stories
___ Prepare library corner

For students using a basal literature textbook or novels:

___ Provide story introductions through modified vocabulary
___ Preteach vocabulary ahead of topic to be read
___ Divide longer stories into shorter segments
___ Use of high-interest, low-vocabulary reading materials
___ Have students keep a personal ongoing dictionary of new/hard-to-spell words

ESOL teacher's signature: _____
Date:_____
Classroom teacher's signature: _____
Date:_____
Parent/guardian's signature: _____
Date:_____

APPENDIX D

~

Blank Weekly
Administrative Planner

Period Planner

School Name: _____ Calendar for Week: _____ Admin. _____

Name: _____

Monday	Tuesday	Wednesday	Thursday	Friday	Saturday
Before School Duty Station:	Before School Duty Station:	Before School Duty Station:	Before School Duty Station:	Before School Duty Station:	Saturday School Y N
Period 1- 8:30–9:25 a.m.	Period 1- 8:30–9:25 a.m.	Period 1- 8:30–9:25 a.m.	Period 1- 8:30–9:25 a.m.	Period 1- 8:30–9:25 a.m.	Notes:
Period 2- 9:25–10:20 a.m.	Period 2- 9:25–10:20 a.m.	Period 2- 9:25–10:20 a.m.	Period 2- 9:25–10:20 a.m.	Period 2- 9:25–10:20 a.m.	
Period 3- 10:25–11:20 a.m.	Period 3- 10:25–11:20 a.m.	Period 3- 10:25–11:20 a.m.	Period 3- 10:25–11:20 a.m.	Period 3- 10:25–11:20 a.m.	
Period 4- 11:25–12:20 p.m.	Period 4- 11:25–12:20 p.m.	Period 4- 11:25–12:20 p.m.	Period 4- 11:25–12:20 p.m.	Period 4- 11:25–12:20 p.m.	
Period 5- 12:25–1:20 p.m.	Period 5- 12:25–1:20 p.m.	Period 5- 12:25–1:20 p.m.	Period 5- 12:25–1:20 p.m.	Period 5- 12:25–1:20 p.m.	
Period 6- 1:25–2:20 p.m.	Period 6- 1:25–2:20 p.m.	Period 6- 1:25–2:20 p.m.	Period 6- 1:25–2:20 p.m.	Period 6- 1:25–2:20 p.m.	
Period 7- 2:25–3:15 p.m.	Period 7- 2:25–3:15 p.m.	Period 7- 2:25–3:15 p.m.	Period 7- 2:25–3:15 p.m.	Period 7- 2:25–3:15 p.m.	
After Sch Duty Station:	After Sch Duty Station:	After Sch Duty Station:	After Sch Duty Station:	After Sch Duty Station:	

Period Planner

School Name: _____ Calendar for Week: _____ Admin. _____

Name: _____

Block Planner

School Name: _____ Calendar for Week: _____ Admin. _____

Name: _____

___ DAY Monday	___ DAY Tuesday	___ DAY Wednesday	___ DAY Thursday	___ DAY Friday	Saturday
Before School Duty Station	Before School Duty Station	Before School Duty Station	Before School Duty Station	Before School Duty Station	Saturday School? Y N
Period ___ 8:45–10:30	Period ___ 8:45–10:30	Period ___ 8:45–10:30	Period ___ 8:45–10:30	Period ___ 8:45–10:30	Reminders this week:
Period ___ 10:35–12:05	Period ___ 10:35–12:05	Period ___ 10:35–12:05	Period ___ 10:35–12:05	Period ___ 10:35–12:05	
Period ___ 12:10–2:10	Period ___ 12:10–2:10	Period ___ 12:10–2:10	Period ___ 12:10–2:10	Period ___ 12:10–2:10	
Period ___ 2:15–3:45	Period ___ 2:15–3:45	Period ___ 2:15–3:45	Period ___ 2:15–3:45	Period ___ 2:15–3:45	
After School Duty Station	After School Duty Station	After School Duty Station	After School Duty Station	After School Duty Station	

APPENDIX E

~

Suggested Pyramid Response to Intervention

SPED
2% of
student
pops.

Tier 3 – SST-Driven
Learning 5% of
student population

Tier 2 – Needs-Based Learning.
In addition to Tier 1, targeted students
are offered additional interventions
and progress monitoring. 20% of
student population.

Tier 1 – Standards-Based Learning.
Tier 1 interventions are for all students.

APPENDIX F

~

Testing Tips

(a combination of tips for both elementary and secondary level)

- Check your senior list twice to make sure that all the students and their eligibility are correct.
- Meet with seniors who have failed one or more portions and with their parents to make sure that they understand the importance of this test. (Some seniors will want to stay home like the exited ones do!) Call home if there is no time to meet.
- Test 11th graders in the portables and the 9th graders inside close to you (the principal). Bring sneakers and plan on walking the halls repeatedly all day, letting the 9th and 10th graders see you constantly.
- Handpick the teachers who are testing kids. Do not allow those teachers who would encourage kids to "Hurry up!" or who have behavior management issues to test. Have them be hall monitors.
- Ninth-grade reading test is the shortest test. Have movies/activities available for students the last couple of hours. The teacher would make a deal with them: They could bring iPods, cards, and so on to use the last 2 hours of school if they would not go fast on the test.
- At 2:45 p.m., pick up the test booklets of the kids who have not finished. Take them to the library. Have them sign in when they get their booklets and sign out when they finish. This will keep the savvy senior from slipping his or her booklet from the stack, then demanding to graduate anyway because it was the school's fault that the booklet was "lost." (This is based on a true story!)
- Have restroom monitors!

- Campus monitors walk classes one at a time to lunch (one in front of the line, one in the back). Students walk back to class with their lunch sacks.
- Principal visits classes after lunch so that she or he can ask students to "Do me a favor . . . take your time with your test."
- Teachers should have a big red sign to flash to a monitor to indicate that they need a break.
- Stagger starting times for test administrators. Have those few who are staying late with the students (who go past 4 p.m.) come in at 9 or 10 a.m. Many students will not finish till late in the day.
- Most important, talk to students early in the week about this expectation: Ask students to test until lunch, go eat, walk away from it for 30 minutes, then go back after lunch and look for mistakes . . . because they are there! We do not want kids returning tests before lunch, if at all possible.
- As we prepare to show the district that we have the best students, principals should spend time testing days talking to students in classes and on the public address system about the confidence that you have in their abilities to knock the top off the test.
- Please remind students that they have worked extremely hard since August and that they will reap the benefits of all the homework and classwork that they have completed so far in the tested areas.
- In the past, 11th and 12th graders usually do well. We really need the 9th and 10th graders to perform at the same level. To help, come up with some type of competition between the 9th and 10th graders to see which grade can perform at the same grade level or better than the 11th and 12th graders. This can be done in elementary and middle school as well.
- Note: Use the names of your school's top three rivals in sports to motivate your students to perform well on the test. That way, they will have bragging rights from now until the end of the summer as they spend time with family and friends.
- In closing, if students are engaged and excited about the opportunity to show their city that the smartest students attend your schools, then the sky will be the limit.
- Please consider having some of your most popular leaders speak with you on the public address system to challenge their classmates. For example, 9th- through 12th-grade officers, student council officers, as well as other established leaders whom you know your students will follow.
- Most important, spend time thanking your teachers for a job well done in preparing the students to make history on their test results.

APPENDIX G

~

Walk-Through Templates

A Learning Audit Tool for Action

Observer:

Teacher:	Observation comments:
Visit 1 T_1	
T_2	
T_3	
T_4	
T_5	
T_6	
Visit 2 T_1	
T_2	
T_3	
T_4	
T_5	
T_6	
Visit 3 T_1	
T_2	
T_3	
T_4	
T_5	
T_6	

Trends noticed within all/most classrooms visited:

Reflection: Is content being covered rigorously to mastery/evidence of PLC collaboration?

Implications: What change have I seen as a result of my leadership action?

Decision on action (timeline—person responsible—action taken):

Things of which to be aware during walk:

Questioning Techniques/Stems

How many at-risk students were called on during the speedwalk?

Was content current as per scope and sequence?

Results will be achieved by addressing the monumental gap between common and effective teaching practices, and between typical and effective supervision.

—*Mike Schmoker (2004)*

Impact Walk Observation Form

Walker: _Jonah Lee_   Date of Walk: _Sept. 16_

Focus of Walk: _Looking for evidence of implementation of the professional development on hands-on, culturally-relevant instruction for second-language students._

Classrooms to be visited- Rooms: _101_ , _123_ , _125_ , _____

Circle duty: Wall Watcher (Talk to Students) Talk to Teacher Look at Student Profiles

Notes from Classroom 1:
Room # _101_

Students were able to talk about their recently-made ancestry math posters. Two students said the research about math and mathematicians from where they came from (both students were from Mayan ancestry in Mexico), was the best part. They mentioned they told their parents about this (it was part of the project to share it at home), and that the parents were thrilled about learning this as well.

Notes from Classroom 2:
Room # _123_

Students mentioned that they enjoyed the math project. One student was from Indian (India) ancestry and said he and his family were amazed to read that India had a huge impact on the numeral system and place value that is still in use 2000 years later.

Notes from Classroom 3:
Room # _125_

Math projects were in various stages of being finished. Most students said they had enjoyed doing the research and could verbalize what they had learned about their ancestry's math and mathematicians.

Notes from Classroom 4:
Room #_____

Impact Walk Consensus Form

Professional Development being analyzed: *hands-on, culturally-relevant instruction for second-language students.*

Did Walkers find evidence of implementation of the professional development?
(Yes)   No
Evidence
From Walls:

There were math projects posted on the walls of almost all classrooms observed. The rubric through which the students worked was also evident on the walls in two of the classrooms.

From Teachers:

Teachers mentioned looking for opportunities to reference the work done on the math posters by their students during their math instruction.
They were excited about the impact the math poster project had on their students. They mentioned they would be looking for additional ways to incorporate more culturally-relevant material into their instruction.

From Students:

The students who were talked with said they enjoyed doing the research on their projects. They mentioned that their families also liked hearing about famous mathematicians from their ancestry. They were able to articulate the types of math that came from "their people", as one young student told us. A couple of students mentioned wanting to do more projects like that.

Ongoing Observation Log for Impact Walks

20__ – 20__

Eagle Jr. High School	Focus of the Impact Walk	Observations	Needed Professional Development Resulting from Impact Walk
Date of Impact Walk: Sept. 12	High-level questioning techniques based on professional development and article study Aug. 27	All four classrooms had question stems posted on the walls. Three out of four teachers were heard to use the question stems as they went through their lesson, checking for understanding. One teacher was working in small groups and rotated around the room. She was not heard to use the question stems.	More classrooms will have to be visited to make sure the high-level questioning continues. Revisiting this important topic on a regular basis should be done every 2–3 weeks until the practice becomes institutionalized.
Sept. 29	ESL strategies based on ESL professional development Sept. 17	All four classrooms showed visual evidence of implementation of the ESL strategies. Environments were print-rich. All four classrooms had evidence of active word walls. Two classrooms were using differentiated instruction as part of their lesson. Two other classrooms had more traditional paper and pencil type of activities.	Review of differentiated instruction is needed since other content area "walkers" have also noticed a lack of differentiated instruction. Professional development will be rescheduled for next week.
Oct. 13	Review of implementation of high-level questioning techniques and ESL strategies	All four classrooms continue to show visual proof of needed ESL vocabulary instruction based on current concept. Some use of high-level sentence stems was heard in two classrooms. Teachers continue to struggle with differentiated instruction.	Differentiated instruction professional development is still needed as well as placing high-level questioning on the PLC agendas to review. Teacher leader team needs to place differentiated instruction as a discussion item for the next meeting.
Nov. 8			
Dec. 1			

Thank you!

School Name and Logo can go here

Campus Best Practices
Implementation Checklist

# of Students: _____
Inclusion teacher?   Y   N
Co-Teaching?   Y   N
Monitoring all students?   Y   N
ESL Teacher/TA?   Y   N

Time in:_____ Time out:_____

_____   Grade/Subject: _____
_____ Monitor: _____ Date: _____

ectations:
ive on Board
ations Communicated
it-Friendly Language
:s Posted Around Room
charts, rubrics, etc.)

2. Classroom Visit:
____ W
____ Focus Walk
____ Speed Walk
____ Current Portfolios Available
____ Profiles Available:
     ____ Current
     ____ Individual ____ Class
     ____ Student Reflections
____ Goal-Setting

Participation/Engagement:
iiven for Response
t 90% Student Engagement
</computer
nance Monitored

4. Student Work:
____ Rigorous – evidence:_____
____ Available & Current
____ Type of student work being done
_____

nal Learning Communities (PLC) Documentation:

e Data
n Planning
on Assessments
sional Development
e Student Work
id Response to Intervention (PRtI)

PLC/Teacher Binder Check:
____ Agendas
____ Meeting Minutes
____ Signatures
____ Action Plan(s)
____ Evidence of:
a. SPED/LEP modifications/
    accommodations/interventions
b. tracking subgroups on success

_____

_____

_____

Filled-Out Campus Best Practices Implementation Checklist Form

Thank

Campus Best Practices
Implementation Checklist

# of Students:_24__
Inclusion teacher? Y **N**
Co-Teaching?   Y **N**
Monitoring all students?
Y N
ESL Teacher/TA? Y N

Campus_MLK Middle School_   Grade/Subject: _7th Grade math_
Teacher: __Ms. Washington__ Monitor: ___Mr. Miller___ Date: _12/02/10_

Time in:_1:23_
Time out:_1:30_

1. Clear Expectations:
_√__Objective on Board
_√__Evpectations Communicated
____Student-Friendly Language
_√__Artifacts Posted Around Room
    (Criteria charts, rubrics, etc.)
Math posters were posted along with
Formula charts. Grading rubric was
posted next to student work! Nice
job on that! Performance Charts also
posted.

2. Classroom Visit:
____Impact Walk
_√__Focus Walk
____Speed Walk
    _√__Current Portfolios Available
    _√__Profiles Available: *most current*
    _√__Current
    _√__Individual ____ Class
    _√__Student Reflections
    _√__Goal-Setting

3. Student Participation/Engagement
____ Time Given for Response
_√__ At least 90% Student Engagement
_√_ Type of student work being done: *Students were in small groups discussing*
_√_ Performance Monitored/At desk   *the math formula chart scavenger hunt.*

4. Student Work   *graphic*
_√__ Rigorous – evidence: *organizers*
_√__ Available & Current   12/2/20__

5. Professional Learning Communities (PLC documentation)
Evidence:
____ Analyze Data
____ Lesson Planning
____ Common Assessments
____ Professional Development
____ Analyze Student Work
____ Pyramid Response to Intervention
     (PRtI)

____PLC _√__Teacher Binder Check:
     ____ Agendas
     ____ Meeting Minutes
     ____ Signatures
_√__ Academic Action Plan(s) *math plan*
_√__ Evidence of: *for this 6 weeks*
     a. SPED/LEP modifications/
        accommodations/interventions
     b. tracking subgroups on success

Comments *Teacher monitored the students as they tried to figure out the*
scavenger hunt. How did you group the students? I saw the group in the back
struggle to find the answers. It didn't look like there was anyone in the group
who could take the lead. Thanks for posting the rubric and period
performance charts! I'm sure you are fueling some good competition between
classes!

References

Abedi, J. (2001). *Assessment and accommodations for English language learners: Issues and recommendations* (Policy Brief No. 4). Los Angeles: National Center for Research on Evaluation, Standards, and Student Testing.

Abedi, J. and Gándara, P. (2006). Performance of English language learners as a subgroup in large-scale assessment: Interaction of research and policy. *Educational Measurement: Issues and Practice* (Winter 2006).

Allen, S. (n.d.-a). *Choosing a business mentor (and getting them to choose you).* Retrieved from http://entrepreneurs.about.com/od/businessmentoring/a/choosinga mentor.htm.

Allen, S. (n.d.-a). *The value of a business mentor: Why every entrepreneur should have one.* Retrieved from http://entrepreneurs.about.com/od/businessmentoring/a/ valueofamentor.htm.

Allen, S. (n.d.-b). *Working with a business mentor: How to create a mutually rewarding relationship.* Retrieved from http://entrepreneurs.about.com/od/businessmentoring/a/ businessmentor.htm.

Archive. (2012). *How to deal with stress.* Retrieved from http://www.archive-au .com_708574/au/h/howtodealwithstress.com/au/2012-11-20.

Bandura, A. (1993). Perceived self-efficacy in cognitive development and functioning. *Educational Psychologist, 28*(2), 117–148.

Center on Education Policy. (2010). *How many schools have not made adequate yearly progress under the No Child Left Behind Act?* Retrieved from http://www.cep-dc.org/ index.cfm?fuseaction=document_ext.showDocumentByID&nodeID=1&Docume ntID=303.

Clouse, R. W. (1999). *Burnout assessment instrument* (rev. ed.). Madison, TN: Matrix Systems, Inc.

Coates, D. (2006). *People skills training: Are you getting a return on your investment?* Retrieved from http://www.2020insight.net/Docs4/PeopleSkills.pdf.

Coutino, M. and Oswald, D. (2004). *Disproportionate representation of culturally and linguistically diverse students in special education: Measuring the problem.* National Center for Culturally Responsive Educational Systems. Retrieved from http://www.ldonline.org/article/S603.

Deutschman, A. (2007). *Change or die.* Retrieved from http://www.fastcompany.com/52717/change-or-die.

DuFour, R. (2004). What is a professional learning community? *Educational Leadership, 61*(8), 6–11.

Eastwood, K. and Lewis, K. (1992). Restructuring that lasts: Managing the performance dip. *Journal of School Leadership, 2*(2), 213–218.

Forbis, A. (2003). *Avoiding the slow burn . . . are you a candidate for professional burnout?* Retrieved from http://www.training.oa.mo.gov/solutionsarchive/solutions4/sym03.pdf.

Gardner, H. (2004). *Changing minds: The art and science of changing our own and other people's minds.* Cambridge, MA: Harvard Business School Press.

Golin, M., Briklin, M., & Diamond, D. (1991). *Secrets of executive success: How anyone can handle the human side of work and grow their career.* Emmaus, PA: Rodale Press.

Guskey, T. (2008). *Practical solutions for serious problems in standards-based grading.* Thousand Oaks, CA: Corwin Press.

Guskey, T. (2011). Five obstacles to grading reform. *Educational Leadership, 1*(69), 16–21.

Jukes, I. and Dosaj, A. (2006). *Understanding Digital Children (DKs).* The Info Savvy Group. Singapore: MOE Mass Lecture.

Knowles, M. (1973). *The adult learner: A neglected species.* Houston, TX: Gulf.

La Celle-Peterson, M. and Rivera, C. (1998). Is it real for all kids? *Harvard Educational Review, 64*(1), 55–75.

Lashway, L. (2002). *Developing instructional leaders.* Eugene: University of Oregon, College of Education, ERIC Clearinghouse on Educational Management.

LearningAce (n.d.). *Stress.* Retrieved from http://learningace.com/doc/1252419/4ea7e564876da9fb106cac44d6a4c8cz/stress.

Learning Points (2000). *Using student assessment data: What can we learn from schools?* Retrieved from http://ncrel.org.library/publications/tools/tools2-03holl.com.

Marzano, R., Pickering, D., & Pollock, J. (2003). *Classroom instruction that works.* Alexandria, VA: ASCD.

Maslach, C., Schaufeli, W., & Leiter, M. (2001). Job burnout. *Annual Review of Psychology.* (ERIC Document Reproduction Service No. ED466023).

McGraw-Hill. (2010). Cell phones in the classroom. *Teaching Today.* Retrieved from http://teachingtoday.glencoe.com/howtoarticles/cell-phones-in-the-classroom.

Michaels, D. (n.d.). *Working with a business mentor: How to create a mutually rewarding relationship.* Retrieved from http://entrepreneurs.about.com/od/businessmentoring/a/businessmentor.htm.

Mindtools.com (n.d.-a). *Locke's Gold Setting Theory: Understanding SMARTGoal Setting.* Retrieved from http://www.mindtools.com/pages/article/new/tTE_87 .htm.

Mindtools.com (n.d.-b). *Stress Management—Start Here!* Retrieved from http:// ww.mindtools.com/pages/article/newTCS_00.htm.

National Association of Secondary School Principals. (n.d.). *Taking action: How assistant principals can advance their careers.* Retrieved from http://www.principals. org/s_nassp/sec.asp?CID=1270&DID=55748.

National Center for Education Statistics. (2007). *Internet access in U.S. public schools and classrooms: 1994–2005.* Retrieved from http://nces.ed.gov/pubs2007/2007020.pdf

National Commission on Excellence in Education. (1983). *A nation at risk.* Washington, DC: U.S. Department of Education.

National Commission on Excellence in Educational Administration. (1987). *Leadership for America's schools.* Tempe, AZ: University Council for Educational Administration.

Newfields, T. (2006). Teacher development and assessment literacy. In *Authentic Communication: Proceedings of the Fifth Annual JALT Pan-SIG Conference.* Shizuoka, Japan: Tokai University College of Marine Science. Retrieved from http:// jalt.org/pansig/2006/PDF/Newfields.pdf.

North Central Regional Technology in Education Consortium. (2010). *Technology: A catalyst for teaching and learning in the classroom.* Retrieved from http://www.ncrel .org/sdrs/areas/issues/methods/technlgy/te600.htm.

Popham, W. J. (2008). *Transformative assessment.* Alexandra, VA: ASCD.

Prensky, M. (2001). Digital natives, digital immigrants. *On the Horizon, 9*(5). Retrieved from http://www.marcprensky.com/writing/Prensky%20%20Digital%20 Natives,%20Digital%20Immigrants%20-%20Part1.pdf.

Resnick, L. B., & Fink, E. (1999). *Developing principals as instructional leaders.* Retrieved from http://www.lrdc.pitt.edu/hplc/Publications/FinkResnick.PDF.

RtI Action Network. (2010). *Building support.* Retrieved from http://www.rtinetwork .org/GetStarted/BuildSupport/ar/BuildingSupport.

Schmoker, M. (2004a). Start here for improving teaching and learning. *School Administrator.* Retrieved from http://www.findarticles.com /p/articles/mi_m0JSD/.

Schmoker, M. (2004b). Tipping point: From feckless reform to substantive instructional improvement. *Phi Delta Kappan, 85*(6), 424–432. Retrieved from http:// www.pdkintl.org/kappan/k0402sch.htm#1a.

Shepard, L. (2000). The role of assessment in a learning culture. *Educational Researcher, 1*(29), 4–14.

Swick, K. (1987). *Student stress: A classroom management system.* Washington, DC: National Education Association. Retrieved from http://www.knea.org/hom/S44. htm.

Texas Education Agency (2011). *2011 Accountability Manual.* Retrieved from http:// ritter.tea.state.tx.us/perfreport/account/2011/manual/manual.pdf.

Texas Education Agency (2003). *2003 Adequate Yearly Progress (AYP) Guide.* Retrieved from http://ritter.tea.state.tx.us/ayp/2003/guide.pdf.

U.S. Department of Education. (2012). *Choices for parents: Description of supplemental educational services*. Retrived from http://www2.ed.gov/nclb/choice/help/ses/description.html.

U.S. Department of Education. (n.d.). *Supplemental educational services*. Retrieved from http://www.ed.gov/nclb/choice/help/ses/description.html.

U.S. Department of Education, Professional Development Team. (1994). *Building bridges: The mission and principles of professional development*. Retrieved from http://www.ed.gov/G2K/bridge.html.

Yingling, M. (2003). The influence of proximal goal-setting instruction on the writing achievement and self-efficacy of 5th grade students. Unpublished doctoral dissertation. Marywood University.